The Age of Chivalry

Manners and Morals
Editor: Richard Friedenthal

The Age of Chivalry

Manners and Morals 1000–1450

Charles T. Wood

Weidenfeld and Nicolson
5 Winsley Street London W1

Text printed by
Ebenezer Baylis and Son, Limited
The Trinity Press, Worcester, and London

Illustrations printed by BAS Printers Limited, Over Wallop, Hants.

SBN 297 74766 5

Contents

39866

Acknowledgments

Because the author of this volume decided to quote only from original sources already existing in translation, so that readers could more readily pursue subjects of particular interest, he is especially indebted to the following persons and firms, all of whom have generously allowed him to quote from works on which they hold copyright. Without their cooperation, the writing of this book would have been that much more difficult.

To Edward Arnold Ltd for Johan Huizinga, *The Waning of the Middle Ages*; Basil Blackwell for Heinrich Fichtenau, *The Carolingian Empire*; Brown University Press for Charles Haskins, *The Rise of Universities*; Cambridge University Press for G. G. Coulton, *Life in the Middle Ages*; Chatto and Windus Ltd for J. Crosland, *Raoul de Cambrai* and A. Kemp-Welch, *Of the Tumbler of our Lady & Other Miracles*; Columbia University Press for Gregory of Tours, tr. E. Bréhaut, *History of the Franks*, Robert of Clari, tr. E. McNeal, *The Conquest of Constantinople*, Odo of Deuil, tr. V. Berry, *De Profectione Ludovici VII in Orientem*, and Andreas Capellanus, tr. J. Parry, *The Art of Courtly Love*.

Also to Eyre & Spottiswoode Ltd and Oxford University Press (American branch) for D. C. Douglas and G. W. Greenaway, *English Historical Documents 1042–1189*, vol. II; the Folio Society for W. S. Scott, *The Trial of Joan of Arc* (published by the Society for its members); Harcourt, Brace & World, Inc. for R. S. Hoyt, *Europe in the Middle Ages*, 2nd ed.; Harper & Row for C. Stephenson and F. Marcham, *Sources of English Constitutional History*; Harvard University Press for H. O. Taylor, *The Mediaeval Mind*, 4th ed.; Professor Philip K. Hitti for his translation of Usāmah Ibn-Munquidh, *An Arab-Syrian Gentleman and Warrior in the Period of the Crusades*; Liveright Publishing Corporation for Manuel Komroff, ed., *The Travels of Marco Polo*; and to The Macmillan Company for F. Luquiens, *The Song of Roland*.

Also to New Directions Publishing Corporations and Mr John Whicher for George F. Whicher, *The Goliard Poets*; Routledge & Kegan Paul Ltd and the

ACKNOWLEDGMENTS

University of Chicago Press for Marc Bloch, *Feudal Society*; Routledge & Kegan Paul Ltd for C. Petit-Dutaillis, *The Feudal Monarchy in France and England* and Anna Comnena, *Alexiad*; Charles Scribner's Sons for O. J. Thatcher and E. H. McNeal, *A Source Book of Mediaeval History*; Sheed and Ward Inc., New York, for John of Joinville, tr. René Hague, *The Life of St. Louis*; The Society of Authors for Dante Alighieri, tr. Laurence Binyon, *Paradiso*; Princeton University Press for A. C. Krey, *The First Crusade: The Accounts of Eye-Witnesses and Participants* and E. Panofsky, *Abbot Suger on the Abbey Church of St. Denis*; the University of Pennsylvania Press for D. C. Munro, *Translations and Reprints form the Original Sources of European History;* Van Nostrand Reinhold Company, a division of Litton Educational Publishing, Inc., Litton Industries, for J. H. Mundy and P. Riesenberg, *The Medieval Town*; les Presses Universitaires de France for R. Latouche, *Textes d'histoire médiévale V^e-XIe siècle*, on which Mundy and Riesenberg based their translation; and, lastly, to Dr W. L. Warren for his 'Peasants' Revolt of 1381, Part Two', which appeared in History Today, XIII (1936).

For further details on dates and places of publication, readers are referred to the Bibioliography and Footnotes.

Prologue
The Formation of Medieval Europe

Few periods have attracted more widespread attention than that of the disintegration of classical civilization, more familiarly known as 'the fall of Rome'. From the Renaissance onwards, scholars have been drawn to study this cataclysm, hoping to distil from its spectacular events lessons from which men in their own day might profit. At the same time few historians have attempted to study the origins of the Middle Ages, and this for understandable reasons. Until recently, all education was classical in orientation, and to men trained in the ways of Virgil and Homer the medieval centuries necessarily appeared as no more than a dark age, the lamentable result of Rome's fall, perhaps, but surely of no consequence in themselves.

Although no reputable historian would hold such parochial views today, the whole subject of the formation of medieval Europe has continued to pose problems, and again for understandable reasons. Before the eleventh century or possibly the twelfth, the Middle Ages lacked anything that might be termed a coherent civilization, so to deal with their earlier development scholars have had to weave together bits and pieces of factual information which do not, in the end, fit together very well as an integrated interpretative whole. Nor should this be really surprising, for one consequence of the fall of Rome was that it so rent the total fabric of European society that hundreds of years were needed to re-knit the tattered remnants of its cultural inheritance into a new garment of civilized comfort.

As the immense amount of literature devoted to the fall of Rome suggests, the subject is both fascinatingly difficult and frustratingly complex. No longer can Roman failure be ascribed simply to Germanic invasions, moral decay and Christianity. Rather, the more we investigate, the more we appreciate the extent to which every aspect of classical civilization was, from the third century on, subjected to a multitude of pressures that none proved able to resist. Economic decay led to the atrophy of towns and a gradual flight to the countryside; central government tended to disintegrate under the impact of reduced revenues, civil war and military ambition; classical, artistic and intellectual standards crumbled before the rise of other and more particularistic ideals. Lastly came Christianity and the Germans, factors that did not so much kill off the Roman world as simply complete its transformation, a process that had long been going on.

The striking feature of all the forces that tended to Rome's destruction is their incompatibility not just with Rome but with each other. To cite only the most obvious example, what had Christianity, the religion of brotherly love, to do with the Germans, a people none too accustomed to turning the other cheek? Both may have served as solvents of the Roman order, but in no way did that circumstance lessen their mutual antagonisms. On the contrary, the very fact that such disparate elements were involved in the destruction of antiquity ensured that any succeeding society would prove incoherent and self-contradictory.

It was not to be expected that these conditions would soon be remedied, for men in the early Middle Ages were as slow to adapt themselves to changing circumstances as they have ever been. Indeed, it can be argued with some cogency that society's failures during this period resulted in no small measure from the continuities that each of its components preserved with its own past. On the one hand, many Roman elements persisted into the new age, safeguarded and protected not only by the Roman origins and upbringing of the vast majority of the population, but also by the fact that the Germans had come, after all, to praise Caesar, not to bury him. The result was that classical ideas and institutions continued to exert an influence in a world that was no longer classical.

On the other hand, much as the Germans admired Caesar and had been drawn to settle on his land in order that they too might share in its advantages, they were nevertheless ill-equipped to serve as guardians of his heritage. Many of the Germanic tribes, notably the Ostrogoths, may have absorbed something of Roman civilization even prior to their rise to political power in the fifth and sixth centuries, but they – and especially the greatest of them all, the Franks – continued to display an outlook on life that reflected the attitudes and organization of a simple tribal society. It is hardly surprising, then, that they should have proved so inept when they tried to take over and maintain the social, political, and intellectual traditions of Rome. So wide was the cultural gulf separating them from those they wished to emulate that there was little hope of their successfully doing so: Germans were not to be made into Romans overnight.

The Christianization of these groups was not a rapid or an easy process. The religion of Christ was initially as much a mystery to the citizens of Rome as it was later to prove to her conquerors. Mistrust of this world and the promise of another to come might confirm its original adherents in the ardency of their faith, but they were, for the most part, men who saw themselves as already separated from the society in which they lived. For those who sensed no such alienation, for those who accepted the world into which they had been born, Christianity must have seemed an impossible religion, implying as it did that conversion necessarily involved a radical and total reorientation of all thoughts and deeds. In the fourth century Constantine and Theodosius first tolerated Christianity and then made it the official and only religion of the Empire; yet the fact of the matter is that these momentous events had surprisingly little impact on most men's habits and outlook. If men flocked to the banner of the crucified Saviour, it was often not because they had truly seen the light, but only because such an outward profession of faith was becoming mandatory for those who desired political and social advancement. The price seemed slight in comparison to the worldly gains to be made.

Chroniclers' accounts of the Germanic acceptance of Christianity suggest the same situation, as witness the marvellous tale of Gregory of Tours about the conversion of Clovis, king of the Franks. It seems that one day the king, though still lost in pagan error, saw certain defeat on the battlefield turned into astounding victory when in desperation he called on Christ to save him. The queen, already a Christian, then summoned St Remi, bishop of Reims, to instruct her husband in the mysteries of the faith:

But the king said: 'I gladly hear you, most holy father; but there remains one thing: the people who follow me cannot endure to abandon their gods; but I shall go and speak to them according to your words.' He met with his followers, but before he could speak the power of God anticipated him, and all the people cried out together: 'O pious king, we reject our mortal gods, and we are ready to follow the immortal God whom Remi preaches.' This was reported to the bishop, who was greatly rejoiced, and bade them get ready the baptismal font. The squares were shaded with tapestried canopies, the churches adorned with white curtains, the baptistery set in order, the aroma of incense spread, candles of fragrant odor burned brightly, and the whole shrine of the baptistery was filled with a divine fragrance: and the Lord gave such grace to those who stood by that they thought they were placed amid the odors of paradise. And the king was the first to ask to be baptized by the bishop. Another Constantine advanced to the baptismal font, to terminate the disease of ancient leprosy and wash away with fresh water the foul spots that had long been borne . . . And so the king confessed all-powerful God in the Trinity, and was baptized in the name of the Father, Son, and holy Spirit, and was anointed with the holy ointment with the sign of the cross of Christ. And of his army more than 3,000 were baptized. His sister also, Albofled, was baptized, who not long after passed to the Lord. And when the king was in mourning for her, the holy Remi sent a letter of consolation which began in this way: 'The reason of your mourning pains me, and pains me greatly, that Albofled your sister, of good memory, has passed away. But I can give you this comfort, that her departure from the world was such that she ought to be envied rather than mourned.'[1]

This mass conversion of the Franks was indeed a wondrous event, and sceptics should be warned to proceed with caution. For there is really no reason to doubt the story that Gregory tells. While we may doubt whether it was actually God who caused the Franks so freely to abandon their mortal gods, it is certainly possible that Clovis appealed to Christ and probable that he accepted Him after he saw that victory was unexpectedly his. Moreover, the sensuous appeal of the new religion, particularly to a primitive mind, is undeniable: candles, hangings, incense, baptismal water – everything combined to suggest a world of the infinite and the mysterious which no Frank had hitherto experienced, but toward which all found themselves ineluctably drawn. Perhaps this attraction is best explained in Bede's familiar story of the conversion of King Edwin of Northumbria who, when he asked why he should accept Christianity, received the following reply from one of his chief men:

The present life of man, O king, seems to me, in comparison of that time which is unknown to us, like to the swift flight of a sparrow through the room wherein you sit at supper in winter, with your commanders and ministers, and a good fire in the midst, whilst the storms of rain and snow prevail abroad; the sparrow, I say, flying in at the door, and immediately out at another, whilst he is within, is safe from the wintry storm; but after a short space of fair weather, he immediately vanishes out of your sight, into the dark winter from which he had emerged. So this life of man appears for a short space, but of what went before, or what is to follow, we are utterly ignorant. If, therefore, this new doctrine contains something more certain, it seems justly to deserve to be followed.[2]

Like that of the sparrow, the world of many of the Germanic peoples was a dark winter from which they were struggling to emerge, and, as the tale suggests, Christianity offered a torch to light the way. Yet that did not mean that the Germans would use it well, any more than the Romans before them. On the contrary, theirs was a different ethic, one which baptism alone could never efface. Clovis may have accepted the religion of charity, but Gregory of Tours can then relate how he plotted the death of all his relatives, only to exclaim at an assembly: 'Woe to me, who have remained as a stranger among foreigners, and have none of my kinsmen to give me aid if adversity comes.' As Gregory adds: 'But he said this not because of grief at their death but by way of a ruse, if perchance he should be able to find some one still to kill.'[3] The case for the uplifting influence of Christianity seems far from proved by the example.

The story is not atypical. Throughout the early Middle Ages incidents abound that illustrate how far society was from understanding and practising the religion it professed. Even as late as the twelfth century, traces of the gulf that could separate the ordinary Christian from the high ideals of his faith are to be found in the *chansons de geste*, whose plots reflect a folk memory of the past, particularly of the reigns of Charlemagne and his immediate descendants. Nowhere is their testimony more vivid than in *Raoul de Cambrai*. Raoul, the hero, has with some justice been called 'a paroxysm of ferocity and impiety', for his career encompasses nearly every imaginable form of savagery and brutality. But despite his shortcomings, Raoul clearly considers himself a Christian and subject to the dictates of the faith, facts that are somewhat startlingly demonstrated after he has burned down a convent filled with nuns, including the mother of one of his squires. Fatigued from this exploit, Raoul returns to his tent, summons his seneschal, and is soon engaged in a difficult exchange of words:

'Prepare me food and thou wilt do me a great service; roasted peacocks and devilled swans, and venison in abundance, that even the humblest may have his fill. I would not be thought mean by my barons for all the gold of a city.' When the seneschal heard this he looked at him in amazement and crossed himself thrice for such blasphemy. 'In the name of Our Lady,' said he, 'what are you thinking of? You are denying holy Christianity and your baptism and the God of majesty. It is Lent, when every one ought to fast; it is the holy Friday of the passion on which sinners have always honoured the cross. And we miserable men who have come here, we have burned the nuns and violated the church and we shall never be reconciled to God unless his pity be greater than our wickedness.' Raoul looked at him and said: 'Son of a slave, why have you spoken to me like that? Why did they wrong me? They insulted two of my squires and it is not a matter for wonder that they had to pay for it dearly. But, it is true, I had forgotten Lent.'[4]

Raoul, sulking, then attempts to submerge his hunger in a game of chess. Thus are Christ's forty days in the wilderness piously commemorated.

Whatever else one may conclude from this story, it hardly suggests a wholly coherent and Christian society. Yet such inconsistencies as Raoul's should not be viewed as solely the product of Germanic inability to grasp fully the principles by which men were to live; on the contrary, the difficulty lay equally with Christianity itself, for just as the Germans were slow to change their age-old ways, Christianity proved hesitant to give up the past.

From its beginnings Christianity had insisted that the true kingdom was not of this world, but lay in that heavenly Jerusalem that men would come to know only after their earthly death. In preparation, however, men in this life were encouraged to abandon secular goals and to infuse all of their daily activities with a love of God that would transform their existence. Otherworldliness was the key to salvation and, needless to say, it was pursued with peculiar intensity as long as Christianity remained a minority sect, persecuted by the hostile majority. Simply to become a Christian required ardency of faith and fierceness of will, but at the same time the lack of concern with this world, which religion implied, provided assurance to the believer since he could view rejection by those around him as nothing more than Providential aid given to help him put aside those temporal concerns which could hinder his quest for salvation. Under these circumstances it is hardly surprising that members of the Church should have been as intense in their spiritual convictions as they were careless of their secular affairs. While in the world, they were not of it.

Nor was this situation changed by Constantine's conversion to Christianity. Although the world was suddenly made Christian, it became in no way less repellent in the minds of the devout. Indeed, in so far as all things were now open to them, the world had become a more dangerous place, filled with temptations that might ensnare the unwary, causing them to lose sight of the ultimate goal. Thus the triumph of Christianity was also a source of crisis; glorious as the victory appeared, it threatened to dilute the purity of the faith by inundating it with a flood of converts whose motives were often suspect. For many, the resulting tension was intolerable, and from the beginning of the fourth century they increasingly sought release from their troubles by physical withdrawal. In this way monasticism was established.

Since monasticism was an institution new to the Church, it might be taken as the sign of some sort of radical reorientation in Christian thought. Nothing could be further from the case. Monasticism represents innovation only in a narrowly institutional sense whereas its real purpose was to preserve continuity and to strengthen that interest in the future life which those most devoted to the faith feared might soon be lost, now that the world had become nominally Christian. Monasticism was little more than a changed response to changed conditions, a replacing of spiritual by physical withdrawal. As such, it illustrates the ways in which a society can resist change by developing new institutions that bend to circumstances while continuing a link to the past.

Nevertheless, the appearance of monasticism had profound consequences for Christianity. So great was its appeal that it tended to attract to its ranks those most deeply concerned with the faith. While the argument must not be pushed too far, it still seems likely that a significant percentage of those whose ability and fervour could have made them the leaders of the drive to Christianize society were instead redirected into monastic channels where their creative efforts might serve as an inspiration for future generations, but where their day-to-day lives had little effect on the activities and outlook of those who had not themselves withdrawn from the world.

As a consequence, just at the moment when the Church desperately needed men of talent to fulfil the promise that Constantine and Theodosius had made possible, it found that such men were increasingly directing their efforts elsewhere. Again it must be emphasized that this was not a universal phenomenon; the lives of the Fathers of the Church show us that. In fact, from the middle of the sixth century onwards many – for example, Gregory the Great, St Augustine of Canterbury, the Irish missionaries – began to issue forth from their cells to participate more fully in the building of a Christian Europe. Even so, the total number available proved infinitesimally small in proportion to the immensity of the problems confronting them;

hence the conclusion that if Christianity long proved unequal to the task, it was partially because of the monastic ideal.

Moreover, the divisive effects of monasticism are but part of the story. Christianity had gained acceptance just as the powers of Rome showed signs of failing. By default the Church was forced to fill the ensuing vacuum, but it was a role for which she was both spiritually and institutionally ill-equipped. In so far as her goals were otherworldly, and in so far as her members tried to live up to the Master's injunction, 'Judge not, that ye be not judged', she found it difficult and contradictory of her mission to intervene in the affairs of the world and to provide a temporal leadership that might replace that of Rome. From her foundation her only concern had been for the care of souls and her institutions had been shaped toward that end; how, then, could she be expected to view with enthusiasm the prospect of having to assume responsibility for spheres of earthly activity she inherently mistrusted?

Lastly, many of Christianity's fundamental beliefs tended to make the Church ambivalent about the intellectual and cultural heritage of classical antiquity. On the positive side, many Christians recognized that the world of thinkers like Plato, Cicero and Seneca did not differ radically from their own. By and large, the pagan philosophers had posited an ordered universe ruled by a supreme being, and they had further assumed that man had a soul, some spark of divinity that might be immortal. Such ideas were perfectly compatible with Christian revelation and, indeed, had considerable attractiveness. This similarity between revealed truth and pure philosophy seemed to validate the realm of reason and suggested that it could be safely employed in exploring some of Christianity's deeper philosophical implications, a project which clearly lay beyond the capabilities of faith alone. Thus, for many Fathers of the Church, theology became a discipline in which the principles of Greek philosophy were applied to Holy Writ in order to explicate its meaning and prove its rationality. Nothing was more natural for men like these, many of whom had been trained in the schools of classical antiquity and only in their maturity became converts to the religion of Christ.

On the other hand, even though the Church was to prove a principal guardian and transmitter of classical culture, few would have predicted it in apostolic times. After all, the Son of God had become flesh to save the world by transforming it; only doom awaited those who remained set in their ways, unprotected by the new armour of Christ, for now the Law, the Prophets, philosophy – everything which had hitherto provided the foundations of human understanding – were declared useless. Faith alone became the road to knowledge, happiness and salvation. As St Paul had put it, 'Christ has made foolish the wisdom of this world'.

Little wonder, then, that so many of the influential people in the early

Church should have shown themselves mistrustful of reason and all pagan learning. Such things had become foolishness although, paradoxically enough, many continued to use them. Tertullian wondered what Athens had to do with Jerusalem and said that he believed because it was impossible; an angel had to caution St Jerome in a dream that he was more a Ciceronian than a Christian; even St Augustine, whose theology was decidedly neo-platonic, found it necessary to warn that pagan thought could be used only if it were never enjoyed for its own sake. As late as the end of the sixth century, Pope Gregory the Great continued to display the same antipathy and suspicion, refusing to apologize for rhetorical and grammatical mistakes because, as he said, 'I account it very far from meet to submit the words of the Divine Oracle to the rules of Donatus'.

In short, if the Germans often exhibited striking cultural conflicts, so did Christianity itself. Although the Germanic successors to Rome became Christian, they retained much of their primitive savagery; although one side of their nature attempted to assimilate the Roman heritage, the other tended inadvertently to destroy it. In the same way, Christianity's mission was to convert, to serve as a light to lighten the Gentiles, but initial success drove many of its ablest adherents to withdraw from the world they were supposed to be serving; the Church employed and preserved much that was best in classical thought, but at the same time so mistrusted that thought that she failed to appreciate its importance. The result was hopeless confusion. Moreover, because conflict and dislocation marked all aspects of society, the argument could be endlessly extended. The Church's attitude may have hindered the growth of an educational structure suited to the needs of the times, but so did the economic decline which denied society the necessary surplus with which to support learning. The Germans' lack of political sophistication may have made it difficult for them to preserve the institutions of the Roman state, but so did the actions of the Romans themselves who had largely destroyed their own creation even before the Germanic rise to power.

To put the case another way, the fall of Rome meant that Romans, Germans and Christians alike were suddenly faced by problems and circumstances radically different from those for which their training had prepared them. Commercial decay and depopulation of the towns created conditions of life totally at variance not only with the requirements of Roman civilization, but with Germanic experience as well. Harried imperial attempts to shore up the tottering system by freezing all men into their occupations led to the appearance of a social structure that accorded poorly both with Roman Law and Germanic custom. These and other antagonisms produced a society that was culturally incoherent and at war with itself, and nowhere does it come more vividly to life than in the pages of Gregory of Tours' *History of the Franks*, written in the last quarter of the sixth century.

Gregory himself was the scion of an old Gallo-Roman senatorial family

The Church Militant

Though the seventh-century Book of Durrow is a Christian work, the small cross at the centre of this carpet page is the only sign of Christianity's impact on the artist's basically pagan and anti-classical conceptions.

The human figure seems to have baffled the Durrow artist when he tried to portray St Matthew.

Under Charlemagne, however, St Matthew was better served, when, with imperial
encouragement, illuminators turned to Roman models for inspiration.

Notre Dame de la Belle Verrière, in Chartres Cathedral. By the thirteenth century, medieval art had become predominantly Gothic in style, and the Virgin had captured men's religious affections.

Surrounded by the symbols of the four Evangelists and supported by the twelve Apostles, Christ remained the ultimate guarantor of salvation (from the central porch of Chartres Cathedral).

peoiis uii ad omem innullo deliquit fz ʒ totus coz
puis siii oispoitoone etiain geneiis nobilitatein eiii

Above : with the Black Death, a new theme entered religious art: the Dance of Death.

Superstitious fears about the devil were prevalent: here (*left*) he is seen tempting a Burgundian heiress (Matthew Paris manuscript, 1225). Flagellants (*right*) scourged themselves to persuade God to end the plague.

Cathedral-building (*above*) took the skills of many crafts and the devotion of many people. At St Julian's of Le Mans (*left*), as elsewhere, the soaring spaciousness of Gothic architecture depended on new discoveries, notably the pointed arch and ribbed groin vaults.

Left : the Cathedral of St Ouen, Rouen. During the fourteenth and fifteenth centuries, Gothic's initial simplicity gave way to a more elaborate and flamboyant style.

The strength of the Church was not to be found solely in its monuments, but also in its personnel, notably its bishops (*top*), abbots and monks (*below right*).

Throughout the Middle Ages, in building and rebuilding churches such as Bosham (*below*) and Westminster Abbey (*above*), men continued to display their faith.

who became, like many of his relatives before him, bishop of Tours and successor to the line founded by St Martin, the former legionary who had shared his cloak with a beggar. Yet the world he describes has little to do with the grandeur that was Rome. Everywhere one sees desolation and torment, the sadness of which is underscored even in Gregory's opening paragraph:

With liberal culture on the wane, or rather perishing in the Gaulic cities, there were many deeds being done both good and evil: the heathen were raging fiercely; kings were growing more cruel; the church, attacked by heretics, was defended by Catholics; while the Christian faith was in general devoutly cherished, among some it was growing cold; the churches also were enriched by the faithful or plundered by traitors – and no grammarian skilled in the dialectic art could be found to describe these matters either in prose or verse; and many were lamenting and saying: 'Woe to our day, since the pursuit of letters has perished from among us and no one can be found among the people who can set forth the deeds of the present on the written page.'[5]

As Gregory's story unfolds, the reader begins to understand why part of the bishop's purpose was to reassure 'those who are losing hope of the approaching end of the world', for so unendurable do life's agonies appear that only the Second Coming and the ending of earthly travail seem to offer any basis for hope. Gregory's Franks are, to put it mildly, a terrifying lot. Clovis can, as we have seen, have his kinsmen murdered and then plead for sympathy as an orphan. When thwarted by one of his warriors who smashes a vase to prevent the king from claiming it, he can cunningly wait for revenge and then, when opportunity arises, plunge his battle axe into the man's head, saying: 'This is what you did at Soissons to the vase.'[6] Nor does life in the court of his grandson seem any more alluring:

Rigunda, daughter of Chilperic, often made malicious charges against her mother and said that she was mistress and that her mother ought to serve her, and often attacked her with abuse and sometimes struck and slapped her, and her mother said to her: 'Why do you annoy me, daughter? Come, take your father's things that I have and do as you please with them.' And she went into the store-room and opened a chest quite full of necklaces and costly jewels. For a long time she took them out one by one and handed them to her daughter but finally said: 'I am tired; you put in your hand and take what you find.' And she thrust in her arm and was taking things from the chest when her mother seized the lid and slammed it down on her head. And she was holding it down firmly and the lower board was pressing against her daughter's throat so that her eyes were actually ready to pop out when one of the maids who was within called loudly: 'Run, I beg you, run; my mistress is being choked to death by her mother.' And those who were awaiting their coming outside rushed into the little room and saved the girl from threatening death and led her out. After that their enmity was more bitter and there were continual quarrels and fighting between them, above all because of the adulteries Rigunda was guilty of.[7]

Treachery, cunning, licentiousness, brutality: these are only a few of the Franks' less attractive qualities. Emotional, quick to anger, direct though often tortuous in their retributive vengeance, this people was poorly suited for assuming the burdens of Roman government and civilization. In one part of his being Clovis might greatly admire Rome and happily don the purple tunic and chlamys of consular office, but how far he and his family were from understanding the true nature of Roman rule is suggested by another incident from Chilperic's reign:

In these days king Chilperic was very sick. When he got well his younger son, who was not yet reborn of water and the Holy Spirit, fell ill, and when they saw he was in danger they baptized him. He was doing a little better when his older brother named Clodobert was attacked by the same disease. Their mother Fredegunda saw they were in danger of death and she repented too late, and said to the king: 'The divine goodness has long borne with our bad actions; it has often rebuked us with fevers and other evils but repentance did not follow and now we are losing our sons. It is the tears of the poor, the outcries of widows and the sighs of orphans that are destroying them. We have no hope left now in gathering wealth. We get riches and we do not know for whom. Our treasures will be left without an owner, full of violence and curses. Our storehouses are full of wine and our barns of grain, and our treasuries are full of gold, silver, precious stones, necklaces, and all the wealth of rulers. But we are losing what we held more dear. Come, please, let us burn all the wicked tax lists. . . .' Then the king repented and burned all the tax books and when they were burned he sent men to stop future taxes. After this the younger child wasted away in great pain and died.[8]

One scarcely knows where to begin when confronted with a tale like this, for how does one analyse, let alone understand, people whose minds work in such strange and wonderful ways? On one level, of course, the logic is clear and unmistakable: sickness implies divine punishment; punishment implies sin; and sin implies taxes that oppress the poor. Hence taxes are abolished, but the child died anyway. Yet more than a naïve view of divine retribution is involved; the unquestioned justice of God's punishment depends on a view of government and society different from anything the Romans had conceived of. Certainly little idea of the *res publica*, of the state, remains; taxes now accrue simply to the benefit of the ruler and no thought is given to the support of public services. Rather than a necessity, taxes are an evil, one to be eliminated should it be thought that the Divinity threatens.

Moreover, the two preceding incidents illustrate perfectly the problem of cultural incoherence. When left to her own devices, Fredegunda shows no compunction about attempting to strangle her daughter in a treasure chest, but when death threatens from causes beyond her comprehension, her character immediately seems to change and her actions become based on a contrary set of premises. There is no integration here; one is dealing with Dr Jekyll and Mr Hyde. And Fredegunda is typical. Clovis himself can

18

dress like a Roman and rule like a savage; Chilperic can tax like a Caesar and repent like a Christian. Although the Frankish army was second to none in its tendency to pillage, Clovis once ordered it to limit its foraging to grass and water because a part of it was passing through the diocese of blessed St Martin of Tours. The order was not, however, at all times observed:

But one from the army found a poor man's hay and said: 'Did not the king order grass only to be taken, nothing else? And this,' he said, 'is grass. We shall not be transgressing his command if we take it.' And when he had done violence to the poor man and taken his hay by force, the deed came to the king. And quicker than speech the offender was slain by the sword, and the king said: 'And where shall our hope of victory be if we offend the blessed Martin? It would be better for the army to take nothing else from this country.'[9]

By stretching the point, one could possibly describe Clovis' action as a deed of brutal charity, but that would be to miss its essential motivation, self-interest. Like Chilperic, who sought to propitiate a wrathful Deity by burning the tax lists, Clovis here seeks success for his army by attempting not to offend St Martin, God's most important agent in Gaul. There is little that is Christian in this; all is pagan, propitiatory superstition. Like the emperor's new clothes, Christianity satisfied the self-esteem of the Franks without in the least transforming the outward appearance of the natural man. And the simile should not be dropped, for it suggests further aspects of the Franks' confusing character. One can easily condemn their lives as nothing more than ruthless barbarism, and yet to do so is to fail to understand the extent to which they, like the emperor, were in the innocence of their pride caught up in circumstances beyond both their comprehension and control. Their tragedy was to live in a world approximating the state of nature, but with none of the joys that Rousseau ascribed to it. The happiness of Rousseau's savage depended, as did Adam and Eve's, on a knowledge limited to conditions as they actually were, whereas the Franks, ignorant as they may have been, were all too aware of the worlds that had been lost to them. Rome was no more, but everywhere her physical ruins remained, silent reminders of a civilization whose skills could no longer be imitated. Little wonder, then, that the men of the Middle Ages should have early begun to regard themselves as dwarfs in comparison to the stature of the giants of classical – and Christian – antiquity.

Haunted by the past and often terrified by the present, men saw little possibility for improvement in this life. At first glance, even the leaders of society offered scant grounds for hope. Rulers like Clovis and Chilperic were hardly enlightened, while intellectuals showed few signs of sophistication. Gregory of Tours, for example, may have been gentler than the Franks he described, but his mental horizons were scarcely less limited. Simple, naïve, credulous – convinced of 'the successes that have come to Christians who confess the blessed Trinity and the ruin which has come to heretics who have tried to destroy the same'[10] – Gregory saw only externals, and even these badly distorted by the simplistic, almost dualistic, assumptions of his faith. Because Clovis had become a Christian he saw no contradiction between the king's brutality and his own conclusion that 'God was laying his enemies low every day under his hand, and was increasing his kingdom, because he walked with an upright heart before Him, and did what was pleasing in His eyes[11]'. Because he saw heresy as man's greatest danger, he was anxious to affirm his own orthodoxy, but could find no way to do so except through an awkward paraphrase of the Nicene Creed.

Nevertheless, culturally incoherent and divided as Frankish society inevitably appears, it contained more elements tending towards eventual unity and integration than toward destruction. First and foremost was Christianity. Badly as men might understand their faith, and poorly as they might live up to its tenets, it had become a necessity for them. Religion gave meaning to life, and meaning was vital in a world gone mad, torn from its foundations, and seemingly without direction and purpose. To know that Christ reigned and that He would reward the just eternally was to know that this sad vale of tears would be transformed; earthly torment was thereby turned into a divine test, thus reassuring the faithful that their trials had a purpose.

And no one illustrates the point more poignantly than Gregory of Tours. For him life was an apocalyptic nightmare, but through thick and thin he held to his convictions. Tyrants raged and 'kings were growing more cruel', but he wrote his history and 'in many localities in the territory of Tours I dedicated churches and oratories and glorified them with relics of the saints. . . '.[12] Even the plague could not surmount his faith:

We lost dear sweet children whom we nursed on our knees or carried in our arms and nourished with attentive care, feeding them with our own hand. But wiping away our tears we say with the blessed Job: 'The Lord has given; the Lord has taken away; the Lord's will has been done. Blessed be his name through the ages.'[13]

Gregory may have been no thinker, but he did his job, building churches, tending the distressed, and providing pastoral care to all those in need. In its way, his was a heroic role, for small was his boat and large was the sea of chaos: rare is the man who will challenge such odds as firmly and calmly as he.

Merely to stress the incoherence of Frankish society is to overlook the extent to which it was in ferment and striving to change. There were few who truly led the Christian life, though many had the desire and tried to respond to the efforts of clerics like Gregory of Tours who brought them the glad tidings of salvation. Often the path was too narrow for their untutored feet, and frequent were the mishaps and disasters along the way, but since life without faith lost its meaning, it was a path that all attempted to tread, however awkwardly, however inappropriately. Although Christianization was to prove a long and painful process, it was not because men were unwilling to be saved.

Nor can it be said that they were unwilling to learn. The glories of the past that haunted them were also a spur and a goad, pushing them on to greater efforts. Because theirs was an ignorance of means, not ends, the Franks could not partake of its bliss, and yet it was precisely their limited knowledge of possible ends that provided an impetus for change. If these were the 'Dark Ages', they were not so by choice. Even a Chilperic, whose skills as a ruler were decidedly limited, was anxious to re-establish learning and culture. He was himself the author of several books, and while Gregory of Tours found his treatise on the Trinity highly heretical and his poetry to 'have no relation of any sort with metre',[14] the real point is not that he failed, but that he tried. So earnest was he in his endeavours – and so sensitive to the problems of language – that he attempted to introduce new letters to the alphabet so that those desiring to learn could more easily acquire a knowledge of reading and an ability to sound out the difficult words.

These facts must temper any interpretation of Frankish society. They do not suggest that Merovingian culture should be regarded as coherent; the mere desire for change could not make its warring elements harmonious. Nevertheless, they imply that society had not reached a dead end, that it would not simply disintegrate and return to conditions of primeval simplicity, leaving no sign that Greece and Rome had ever existed. Certainly there would be no return to the past, no rigid recreation of classical antiquity, for the disunity of sixth-century Gaul had arisen largely because it had too many pasts, all with independent traditions, and all at odds with each other. Roman, German, and Christian alike all had their sources of strength and reasons for being, and to favour one at the expense of the others would have been to embark on a foolhardy and impossible mission. Since they were there, they could not be denied. Each would have to accept the others and learn to live with them.

In saying this, we have arrived at the key to European manners and morals as in the Middle Ages. Medieval manners and morality had no simple origins, but owed their character to a variety of backgrounds that were harmonized and synthesized only over the course of centuries. The nature of the problem can be seen in Merovingian Gaul, and that, possibly, is its true importance. Roman culture suggested a world of measured, finite order in which law and rationally apprehensible proportion regulated man's conduct and aspirations. It was a world in which abstractions could exist – state, philosophy, justice, virtue – yet one whose principal concerns, even in abstraction, were with the here-and-now and with what man could do on his own.

How different the Christian heritage. It told men that this globe was no more than a vale of tears, a testing ground and way station on the road to eternity. No longer did man's reason have merit in and of itself; it was sinful and defective, in need of that aid which only God's grace and revelation could give. Faith and love were to take precedence over law, and man was to abandon earthly goals in favour of heavenly ones, a process that involved the abandonment of self and the acceptance of an order above and beyond all human and temporal proportions.

Lastly, the German inheritance. Like the Romans, the Germans lived in the here-and-now, but in a world almost totally devoid of those reasoned abstractions that gave Roman life its substance and being. Germanic law had no principles or legal fictions to lend it universal applicability; there was no legislator or code to appeal to for redress of grievances. Instead, law was concrete and customary; it depended on man's memory of the past and insisted that precedent was to govern the actions of the present. No state existed in the Roman sense; abstract authority was replaced by personal leadership while the ability to command flowed not from one's office, but from one's success in getting others to recognize an individual and personal subordination.

The German outlook did not much resemble the Christian either. Its virtues were those of the warrior, and its ethic found no room for the notion that the meek should inherit the earth. True, the Germans did not inhabit a purely secular world; all aspects of nature were infused with divinity, but of a kind that bore little relationship to the Christian. Goblins and witches roamed through the land, unclean and unnatural spirits that had to be propitiated through sacrifice and incantation lest they visit disaster upon the innocent and unwary. The gods – indeed, initially even the Christian God – were sought out and worshipped not because they brought happiness and salvation, but because they brought victory and power.

While it is true, as the French like to point out, that to make an omelette you must break some eggs, one tends unconsciously to assume that the eggs will all come from the same kind of bird. But what if they are taken from eagles, pelicans, and snapping turtles in equal proportion? What sort of omelette will one have then? That was the problem of the early Middle Ages, and the wonder is that anything at all could be made from the mess.

Nevertheless, progress came, albeit slowly. The three centuries separating Clovis (481–511) from Charlemagne (768–814) saw gradual and then rapid change, and it has often been claimed that with the appearance of the Carolingian dynasty in the eighth century, and the imperial coronation of Charlemagne in 800, medieval civilization took on its essential characteristics. Yet, like all generalizations, this one is a bit wide of the mark, for to accept it completely would be to overestimate the achievements of Charlemagne and his age. Great as they undoubtedly were, they must be seen in proper perspective.

On the positive side, no one would dispute the idea that the Carolingians ruled over a people whose society and culture had become considerably more coherent than those of the Merovingians. Most notable was Christianity's further penetration into men's unconscious assumptions and attitudes. No longer was the ruler, like Clovis, merely a glorified warrior-chieftain; with the coronation of Pepin by Pope Stephen II (754) the Frankish kings became for the first time God's anointed, His vicar on earth, responsible at the Judgment Day both for his personal conduct and that of his subjects. Germanic personalism was thereby infused with Christian content and political power was increasingly felt to carry with it a sense of public obligation such as the Merovingians had never experienced.

Moreover, these proved more than rhetorical or purely symbolic developments. As Charlemagne put it in explaining his imperial duties to Pope Leo III:

My part it is, in accordance with the aid of divine piety, to defend on all sides the holy church of Christ from pagan incursion and infidel devastation abroad, and within to add strength to the Catholic faith by our recognition of it. Your part it is, most holy father, having raised your hands to God, like Moses, to aid our arms, in order that, by your intercession, God granting and leading us, the Christian people may everywhere be always victorious over the enemies of its holy name.[15]

There is in this statement a great deal to which even a Clovis could have subscribed; in particular, the emphasis on warfare and victory, on the necessity of divine aid for imperial success, is one with which any Merovingian would have agreed. But Charlemagne also strikes a new note, for when he points out that his duty is to defend the Church and to strengthen the faith, he is assuming positive religious obligations far different in scope from the negative approach of the Merovingians symbolized in Clovis' prohibition of pillage in the diocese of Tours. No longer are God and His saints merely to be bought off; they must be actively aided.

From the beginning of his reign Charlemagne showed himself anxious to live up to his Christian duties. His legislation regulated the life of the clergy, provided for the creation of episcopal schools, and specified how churches were to be built and what books they were to contain. To cap this quest for moral and spiritual renewal, he established a palace school at Aachen and staffed it with talent attracted from all over Europe. In return, the court scholars proclaimed Charlemagne the new David, both ruler and shepherd to his flock, and that the emperor himself was not unmindful of the obligations involved is suggested by the oath he sought from all his male subjects in 802, an oath which, among other things, bound them 'to live entirely in the holy service of God in accordance with his own promise, because the lord emperor is unable to give to all individually the necessary care and attention'.[16]

Here another aspect of the Carolingian period's greater cultural coherence begins to emerge because, while Germanic personalism still strongly pervades Charlemagne's apparent belief that he ought, if able, individually to provide for the Christian instruction of each of his subjects, no longer does it seem to war with those Christian and Roman assumptions that the original Germans had found so hard to grasp. Indeed, possibly one of Charlemagne's most significant policies was that which saw the harnessing of personalism to the purposes of the state. The Carolingian Empire, although organized only in the most rudimentary fashion, nevertheless had its complement of public officials to preserve order and justice. Yet, as Merovingian rule had shown, the Franks did not readily understand or obey a purely public authority; on the contrary, even the counts themselves often were hesitant to observe the commands of the king. The Carolingians, and particularly Charlemagne, solved this problem by insisting that each of their officials and members of the army swear individual and private oaths of personal allegiance. Increasingly at the end of the eighth and the beginning of the ninth centuries, leading land-holders, even those who enjoyed no public office, were likewise encouraged to take a similar oath. In this way all those who possessed power or who might otherwise threaten the stability of government were brought into a network of personal dependence and obligation.

Personal ties the Franks could grasp, and this system of royal vassalage, as it came to be called, provided a means whereby the non-abstracting Germanic mind could be made to serve ends larger than self-aggrandizement and greed. Because the Carolingian state emphasized its Christian foundations and Christian mission, and because it relied for authority on private oaths of personal subordination, it did not much resemble the Roman *imperium* it claimed to succeed and renew. But that is not the point to be made. Rather, the real point is that for the moment the system worked. More successfully than the Merovingians, the Carolingians brought together the diverse elements of their fragmented heritage and wove them into a relatively cohesive whole.

At least, that is the view of those who see the age of Charlemagne as the period in which medieval civilization began to flower. It is not easy to deny the essential justice of their case: Charlemagne's imperial coronation established the medieval empire while underlining the religious character of political power; his palace school and educational reforms lay at the heart of the so-called Carolingian renaissance and of all later revivals in learning; his encouragement of vassalage led in time to the development of the whole feudal system. And this is but part of the story; the more one analyses the following centuries, the more one appreciates how much they owe to Carolingian beginnings.

Nevertheless, while all this is true, possibly the most striking feature of the Carolingian period is simply its brevity. Within seventy-five years of Charlemagne's death Europe was again in chaos: the empire had crumbled, seemingly into nothingness; learning and education had largely disappeared and were tenuously preserved only in widely scattered monasteries; everywhere the land was given over to depredation, carnage and strife, the consequences of civil war and renewed barbarian invasion, this time from the Muslim South, the Hungarian East, and especially the Scandinavian North. The whole of Charlemagne's creation – all those things for which his age had justly proclaimed him great – lay utterly in ruins.

These facts alter one's sense of the Carolingian achievement. If Charlemagne and his line were the true founders of medieval civilization, the catastrophic disasters of the later ninth and tenth centuries make it clear that this was a matter of chance, not design. For the Carolingians' structure was but poorly planned, and the ease with which their accomplishments were overturned gives evidence of the extent to which their synthesis of opposing cultural forces was tentative, incomplete, and shot through with tensions.

To put the argument in more metaphorical terms, the Carolingians proved better quarriers than builders. They showed sound judgment in selecting durable materials of excellent quality, but they lacked the architectural skills needed to put them together. Thus, when storm clouds arose, their structure collapsed, and even though most of its materials were again to be used when it later became possible to rebuild, the edifice that arose bore little relationship to anything the Carolingians had ever planned. Elements of their craftsmanship were everywhere apparent, but other architects were in charge of the work. Able as the Carolingians undoubtedly were, they resembled the Merovingians in so far as they too failed to find a viable solution for the problems that had beset society at least since the fall of Rome. This is not really surprising, for it is another example of the continuity of history and of the difficulties inherent in attempting to alter its path. On the one hand, men like Pepin and Charlemagne displayed genius in manipulating their confusing cultural inheritance: by emphasizing such things as the Germanic personal tie, the Roman sense of government and order, and the Christian belief in the religious foundations of all knowledge and power, they brought to the fore precisely those aspects of their tradition that were to prove most durable and appealing.

On the other hand, it would be difficult to describe the Carolingians as truly creative. Like most men, they were partially captive to the values of the society into which they had been born, and their vision was limited by the boundaries that those values seemed to impose. Neither for them nor for their subjects did it appear possible to overthrow the ideas and institutions of the past, since to have done so would have been to abandon all those social and cultural presuppositions which shaped their lives. As Alcuin expressed it: 'We are dwarfs at the end of all time; there is nothing better for us than to follow the teaching of the Apostles and the Gospels. We must follow these precepts instead of inventing new ones or propounding new doctrine or vainly seeking to increase our own fame by the discovery of newfangled ideas.'[17] Minds like this were hardly attuned to the pressing need for change, and if Alcuin, the greatest teacher of Charlemagne's court, could have held such views, who is to imagine that his master would have gainsaid him?

For, many as are the myths about Charlemagne, once the layers of legend and romance are removed, he emerges a thoroughly conventional, though highly impressive, man of his age. Every inch the warrior – and at over six feet he had more inches than most – he gloried in the endless military expeditions that brought him renown. Thirty-three years were spent in subduing the Saxons, while shorter campaigns were conducted in Aquitaine, Italy, Spain, Brittany, Bavaria, Bohemia, and Pannonia. If men admired Charlemagne in his own day, it was in large measure because of the prowess and skill with which he led his armies and brought victory to the Franks.

It cannot be said, however, that Charlemagne was a prototype of the modern soldier-intellectual. Much as the emperor admired and encouraged those who worked with their minds, he himself showed little talent for it, although he unquestionably tried:

The King spent much time and labour with [Alcuin] studying rhetoric, dialectics and especially astronomy. . . . He also tried to write, and used to keep tablets and blanks in bed under his pillow, that at leisure hours he might accustom his hand to form the letters; however, as he did not begin his efforts in due season, but late in life, they met with ill success.[18]

Perhaps no one has caught Charlemagne's essential character more successfully than his contemporary, Einhard, from whom the quotation above. Writing ten or fifteen years after the emperor's death, he frequently glosses over some of his hero's less attractive attributes, but at the same time, for all its glorification, the portrait he paints retains the ring of truth:

Charles was large and strong, and of lofty stature. . . . In accordance with the national custom, he took frequent exercise on horseback and in the chase, accomplishments in which scarcely any people in the world can equal the Franks. He enjoyed the exhalations from natural warm springs, and often practised swimming. . . . He used not only to invite his sons to his bath, but his nobles and friends, and now and then a troop of his retinue or bodyguards, so that a hundred or more persons sometimes bathed with him.

He used to wear the national, that is to say, the Frank, dress – next his skin a linen shirt and linen breeches, and above these a tunic fringed with silk; while hose fastened by bands covered his lower limbs, and shoes his feet, and he protected his shoulders and chest in winter by a close fitting coat of otter or marten skins. Over all he flung a blue coat, and he always had a sword girt about him. . . . He despised foreign costumes, however handsome, and never allowed himself to be robed in them, except twice in Rome, when he donned the Roman tunic, chlamys, and shoes. . . .

Charles was temperate in eating, and particularly so in drinking . . . but he could not easily abstain from food, and often complained that fasts injured his health. He very rarely gave entertainments, only on great feastdays, and then to large numbers of people. His meals ordinarily consisted of four courses, not counting the roast, which his huntsmen used to bring in on the spit; he was more fond of this than of any other dish. While at table, he listened to reading or music. The subjects of the readings were the stories and deeds of olden time: he was fond, too, of St Augustine's books, and especially of the one entitled *The City of God*. He was so moderate in the use of wine and all sorts of drink that he rarely allowed himself more than three cups in the course of a meal. In summer, after the midday meal, he would eat some fruit, drain a single cup, put off his clothes and shoes, just as he did for the night, and rest for two or three hours. He was in the habit of awaking and rising from bed four or five times during the night. While he was dressing and putting on his shoes, he not only gave audience to his friends, but if the Count of the Palace told him of any suit in which his judgment was necessary, he had the parties brought before him forthwith, took cognizance of the case, and gave his decision, just as if he were sitting on the judgment seat.[19]

Striking as this description may be, it is nevertheless one of a man whose lack of sophistication is everywhere apparent. Simple, gregarious, restless and direct, Charlemagne was surely the natural leader of his people, but hardly one to suggest radically new and inventive approaches to their difficulties. In dress, habits and outlook he retained most of the characteristics of his more savage Frankish forebears, and for all his questing after empire, for all his intense support of religion and learning, he appears to have possessed no introspective qualities, no self-awareness that might have enabled him to rise above the restricting assumptions of his cultural heritage. On the contrary, like Alcuin he was content to follow the teaching of the past rather than seek to increase his own fame by the discovery and propagation of 'newfangled ideas'.

When viewed in this light, Einhard's *Life of Charlemagne* becomes less a paean of praise to the accomplishments of a great man than a testimonial to the remarkably small impact of those accomplishments on men's cultural attitudes. For if Charlemagne himself could remain so largely unaffected in habits and outlook by the changes he strove to effect, there is little reason to suppose that his subjects were any more likely to abandon traditional ways. In terms of contemporary aspirations and needs the Carolingian achievement was often irrelevant because, aside from the simple restoration of political order, it failed to benefit everyday living. Religion could be reformed, education revived, and empire restored, but so small was the group involved in these changes that they seemed to exist in a world apart.

In a sense, then, the brilliant successes of the Carolingian period were hothouse creations that owed their sustenance solely to the personal care and attention of the ruling house, and not to the natural environment. In so far as this was true, they had an air of unreality about them, an artificiality not unlike that of Marie Antoinette and her coterie playing milkmaid at Versailles. Thus, while Charlemagne might wish to bring back the grandeur that was Rome, in fact no one had a very clear idea how this was to be done. If a suitable palace church was to be erected at Aachen, it had to be painfully copied from the Byzantine church of San Vitale in Ravenna, an edifice whose spatial complexities its German imitators failed totally to grasp. In the same way, the representational art of manuscript illuminations became increasingly classical and Romanized in intent, but nevertheless betrayed a tension in execution resulting from an inability to understand the form; Germanic artists, raised in schools far different from that of Rome, were as yet incapable either of working wholly within the classical mode or of synthesizing effectively the two traditions. Much that they produced is charming, but it is also imitative and flat, for it lacks that depth of feeling which only mastery of a medium can achieve.

Moreover, this kind of cultural strain was far from being limited to the field of artistic endeavour. Every aspect of Carolingian life displayed similar tendencies. Often as ruler and prelate might stress the religious foundations of power, few were the men who fashioned their actions accordingly. With the introduction of the stirrup in the eighth century, an innovation that provided security and stability in the saddle, the Frankish warrior became increasingly a cavalryman, but his new armament did not immediately combine with Christian conceptions to make him into the crusading, chivalric knight of medieval romance. On the contrary, he remained very much the undisciplined, rapacious barbarian of Merovingian times, convinced that right was to be found not in the Church, but solely in the strength of his good right arm.

The spread of vassalage did not markedly alter the situation, for it too was almost entirely lacking in those vaguely religious sentiments that were later to permeate the rhetoric of feudalism. An oath of homage established a personal relationship, nothing more, and while it was assumed to be based on a love and respect that were both mutual and lasting, it arose in a purely practical and Germanic context almost totally devoid of elements from the other traditions that were also a part of the Carolingian heritage. Indeed, even though private personal ties had long been a feature of Frankish society, the use to which they were put by Pepin and Charlemagne led quickly to a new type of tension. In previous centuries vassalage, though recognized, had carried with it such an implication of degradation that men had been tempted to enter into the relationship only in cases of necessity. Under Pepin and Charlemagne, however, when even the mightiest were required to give homage to the king, the situation became more ambiguous. On the one hand, the prestige of a Charlemagne and the universality of the obligation tended eventually to make vassalage a respectable condition, but on the other, this new application of a formerly degrading relationship proved initially a source of enormous strain within the body politic as counts and dukes, notably Tassilo of Bavaria, understandably resisted the introduction of what they regarded as an infringement on their honoured positions.

Then too, the switch to cavalry and the spread of networks of vassalage helped produce a kind of social differentiation previously unknown. Etymologically 'Frank' means 'free', and the Franks had always viewed the right to bear arms and to fight as the badge of their freedom. By 800 this was ceasing to be true. The cost of the new armaments – horse, saddle, weapons, and extensive protective armour – proved beyond the means of most men. Far from expecting all Franks to fight in the army, Charlemagne increasingly sought service from only a small proportion of his poorer subjects, with maintenance to be provided by the rest. Further, since those most loyal to the ruling house also frequently lacked the necessary resources, the Carolingians from the time of Charles Martel began to endow them with royal and ecclesiastical lands from which they might derive the revenues needed to meet the new military requirements. Lastly, Charlemagne encouraged the powerful and wealthy to acquire and maintain vassals, men who would be able to fight at their side in the royal army.

The result of these policies was the appearance of a social complexity unknown to the Merovingians. As those on the bottom of the economic ladder lost their ability, and indeed their right, to fight, they were ever more sharply distinguished from those who stood above them. Simultaneously, a hierarchy began to emerge even among people of consequence, if only because the extension of vassalage tended to place them in ladders of personal dependence and implied subordination.

In so far as this growing differentiation reflected actual divisions of labour, it may be taken as a proof of Carolingian social advance and a sign that the simplicity of organization so characteristic of earlier times was proving inadequate to the needs of an increasingly complex society. Yet the dislocations involved in these changes were clearly enormous, and before the new structure could be established on firm and peaceful foundations, the whole society was to be swept away in a maelstrom of civil war and invasion.

The Carolingian period was a time of hopeful beginnings, but beginnings that were never allowed a full chance of development. Doubtless civilization would have assumed a different cast had not the later ninth and early tenth centuries seen such terrors and anarchy; doubtless too a coherent culture would have that much sooner appeared. But these things were not to be. From the 830s onward Western Europe and England became a place of violence and devastation, and although many of the individual aspects of Carolingian organization and culture survived the storm, the society that emerged toward the end of the tenth century bore little relationship to anything that had come before. Central authority had largely disappeared; counts and dukes, previously public officials, had usurped their offices and the lands that went with them, making them into hereditary family possessions; in the same way, lesser men had risen against the counts and dukes, doing to them what they had done to the king. Political power – such as existed – was thus badly fragmented and exercised almost entirely as a purely private and landlord right. Kingship and ties of vassalage remained, but both had become attenuated and meaningless, except possibly in Germany where the later tenth century saw the empire revived after a lapse of nearly one hundred years. The education and art that had made the surface of Carolingian life so brilliant and attractive was now lost or relegated to safe retreats and border areas of Europe, notably Germany again, but also the British Isles. Lastly, while religious faith grew ever stronger, the actual structure of the Church itself lay seemingly in ruins.

In the tenth century, it might have appeared that society and culture were entering a new dark age. Yet, much as men might bewail their fate and fear that the reign of Antichrist was nigh, changes were occurring beneath the surface that boded well for the future. For the destruction wrought by the invasions was less universal than commonly assumed, and innovations were being introduced, particularly in agriculture, that would eventually improve the material underpinnings of society, thus making possible in an economic sense the flourishing civilization of the following centuries. And it was precisely during this period that the diverse components of the European cultural heritage began at last to fuse and take on coherence. No royal policy accounts for this change, and no artificial stimulation hastened its creation. Rather, what seems to have happened (though details and causes will never be known for a certainty) is simply that the terrors of the ninth and tenth centuries served as a refiner's furnace, consuming the dross and leaving only those elements whose strength best suited them to be the building materials of the high Middle Ages.

Thus, as the year 1000 approached, Europe was prepared to rebuild. By then the fall of Rome had receded into the far-distant past, an event whose relationship to the present was of little concern. Yet the fact of the matter is that the five intervening centuries were scarcely more than a transitional period in which the Middle Ages were still fundamentally engaged in solving the problems and healing the schisms that the collapse of antiquity had entailed. After 1000, however, came a change in direction and mood: the age of chivalry was beginning.

Part 1

The World of the Millennium

1 The Peasants

In the Middle Ages, everything begins with the land. We accept easily enough the fact that medieval man lived in an agricultural society, that his existence was bounded by a world of fields, meadows and forests, but all too seldom can we visualize what life in such a world might have been like. Few towns, surely, and little commerce and industry, but beyond that our minds can conjure up only visions of country fairs, sylvan dances and happy haying parties wending their way through verdant fields. Thus does an urban society search out its lost innocence in the past.

Around the year 1000, however, such innocence would have been difficult to find. True, the invasions from Scandinavian North, Muslim South and Magyar East had stopped, and there were signs, especially in England and Germany, of a return to stability and order. Nevertheless, conditions were generally appalling, and such improvements as the ending of the invasions had brought were for the moment no more than palliatives that took the sharpest edge off the grim realities of life. Could we return to the world of the millennium, our first impression would doubtless be of a Europe practically untouched by the hand of man. And this impression would not be totally inaccurate, for population levels were low: probably less than a million in England, no more than six to eight million in France. Everywhere stretched the forest – dark, impenetrable, brooding – which cut off the scattered human settlements from one another and turned each community inward on itself. Here, it might seem, was opportunity, a virgin land for the asking that needed only to be cleared and put to the plough for man to realize its abundance. But it was not so, at least not in terms of the capacities of the time. In the nineteenth century pioneers might venture forth and through their toil open up new worlds in America and Australia, but in the tenth and eleventh such challenge and opportunity could hardly be met. Though conditions were soon to change, for the moment they dictated a life of Malthusian despair.

The grim truth was that, given the agricultural techniques of the age, Europe was in a state of incipient or actual overpopulation, and there was

C

no surplus on which a growing society could be fed. In modern times few live by the plough, for with fields well fertilized and machines to till them the farmer brings forth a crop sufficient for himself and scores of others. In the tenth century the land proved less generous, and the peasant, for all his labours, was fortunate indeed if he could wrest an adequate return from the soil even for his own modest needs.

In no other epoch, perhaps, was the spectre of famine more real. To exhume graves from the period is an experience never to be forgotten; they yield skeletons whose bones are fearfully deformed by rickets and whose worn teeth give mute testimony to a diet which must have included grass as one of its principal staples for years on end. Bark and roots were the edibles when times were hard, and even in the best of days acorn bread was not uncommon. Famine is never a pretty thing, but its full horror is lost on the urban dweller who can from his circumstances never know just how viciously it taunts and teases the peasant. For those in a city, famine comes when the shops run out: one starves because there is nothing left to eat. For the peasant, however, the irony is that he starves with food still on hand, but food that cannot be eaten since it is the seed for the coming year, seed that is his only hope for future survival, assuming he could live so long as to be able to plant and harvest it. How does it feel to watch one's children starve, knowing that there is seed-corn readily available? That is a question that all too many men in the tenth century could have answered.

Incredible as such conditions may seem, they were the inevitable result of having to confront a harsh and unyielding nature with primitive and inadequate tools. History tells us that Europe entered the Iron Age in late preclassical times, but that assertion is unprovable from the farm implements of the year 1000. The peasant still lived primarily in an age of wood: iron, when available, was much too valuable to waste on agriculture: it was for weapons, and was reserved to those whose station placed them far above the menial tillers of the soil. As a result, when the soil was tilled, it was tilled with wood – possibly tipped with metal, but more usually simply hardened by fire. Sometimes this wood took the form of a plough, frequently that of a hoe, but in neither case was the tool very effective. It scratched at the earth even as the earth scratched back at it, wearing down the point on which survival so narrowly depended. Nor was this plough the wheeled machine with share and mortarboard that became familiar in later centuries: it was the so-called swing-plough, a simple, triangular device such as is still to be seen in photographs from far-distant and underdeveloped parts of the world.

These tools, bad enough in themselves, also led to a number of less obvious, though no less unfortunate, consequences. Not least among them was medieval man's inability to cultivate the more fertile soils. Rich loam, moist and clayey, might have provided a better return, but a swing-plough cannot handle it. Instead, only the lighter soils could be put to seed, and these, so lacking in essential nutrients, could bring forth only a stunted growth. Although by the thirteenth century farming manuals would insist that there should be a tenfold return on every seed planted, it seems doubtful whether the peasant three centuries earlier could count on much more than a four- or fivefold return even in the best of years.

In all of this there were obvious elements of a vicious circle. The revival of society depended entirely on an increase in agricultural productivity, on the creation of a food surplus that would enable a significant proportion of the population to engage in something other than agriculture. Commerce, industry, and the arts cannot flourish if their practitioners cannot be fed, as they could not be in the world of the millennium. Over ninety per cent of the people had to farm simply to survive, and their level of efficiency was so low that it seemed impossible to break free of the chain of limiting circumstances that threatened to bind all men perpetually to the land.

One has only to consider the situation to appreciate its perplexities. With iron tools it might have been possible to raise production, but this could be done only by freeing men from the plough who could fell the timber, dig the ore, and run the smelters and smithies needed to produce those tools. This was impossible. Similarly, if more land could have been opened to cultivation and if each peasant could have increased the acreage that he personally tilled, a surplus might have appeared. Even the intensive fertilization of existing fields would have had the same effect. Here again the peasant confronted a series of interrelated problems. Without iron tools he could not readily plough more land, and he was further hindered in this endeavour by his primitive methods of harnessing farm animals, generally oxen. Yokes were practically unknown, and most peasants were content, like the Romans before them, to harness their draught animals with simple thongs of leather passed around their necks. As a result, rapid ploughing and the ploughing of heavy soils became even more difficult since to increase the amount of strain on a beast beyond modest levels was to risk either strangulation or cutting-off of the blood supply to the brain.

Moreover, low yields also meant that there was never enough corn or fodder with which to carry horses and cattle through the winter. Although it would be hard to prove, it seems likely that all the feasting associated with mid-winter holidays such as the twelve days of Christmas arose largely because late December was about as long as men could afford to keep their cattle: the vast majority of each herd had to be slaughtered, and, in the absence of refrigeration and other means of preservation, rapidly consumed. The spitted ox slowly turning over the yule log has become the symbol of abundance, jollity and good cheer, but in its origins this custom gave testimony to far different conditions.

Few animals, then, survived the winter, and such as did were apt to be sick, half-starved, and covered with mange, not very promising beasts with which to start spring ploughing. And what is more, there were never enough to meet the need. In turn, this inadequacy led to two further consequences, a dependence on human muscle power in situations where animals would have been vastly more efficient, and a shortage of manure with which fields could have been fertilized to increase their yield. Because of this latter problem peasants were forced frequently to rest their land, allowing half of it to lie fallow in any given year lest overuse lead to soil exhaustion.

Yet, if material conditions lay at the root of many hardships, peasant attitudes and assumptions had not a little to do with the situation. On this subject there is little direct evidence, since an illiterate population can leave no records with which to inform the future; nevertheless, the main outlines are clear, both from indirect, often archaeological, sources and from the conclusions of those working today on the problems of underdeveloped countries which not infrequently show a maddening resistance to the process of modernization. By and large, most peasant cultures – and certainly that of the late tenth century – can be characterized as being 'tradition-directed'. These cultures place little importance on innovation; indeed, invention is scorned and even feared as a threat to the traditional way of life. Society organizes itself on the basis of precedent and custom, often encumbered and hedged about with religious sanctions, and anyone who would question the dictates of the past runs the risk of encountering the wrath both of man and of God.

Sociologists have concluded, and rightly, that the key element in the preservation of a tradition-directed society lies in its child-rearing patterns. Raising children is so ordinary a task that we seldom stop to consider the principles on which it is based: we are usually content to assert that the training of the young is designed to make them, when adult, into useful and productive members of society. What we do not appreciate in saying this is that different societies have different needs and hence will create different ways of educating their youth to their future responsibilities.

In the twentieth century, for example, one of the principal dilemmas faced by any parent is how to rear a child whose future occupation is largely unknown: so complex and mobile is the society we have created that those reaching maturity have the opportunity, if properly trained, of choosing their careers from an almost infinite spectrum of possibilities. Not surprisingly, then, our child-rearing places great emphasis on an educational system that will teach the young not how to do anything in particular, but how to think in the abstract, marshal evidence, and reach valid conclusions no matter what the subject. Only in this way can each child be prepared to cope with the uncertain challenge of the future.

In the world of the millennium parents faced no such dilemmas. The very simplicity of society eased their task, for the role of each child from birth (assuming he survived) was already apparent. If he were the son of a peasant, he too would become a peasant: there was no other choice open to him. Abstraction and thought were not for him; rather, from earliest youth he was instructed in the concrete details of farming, in how the oxen were harnessed, the fields ploughed, and the grain winnowed from the chaff. From an early age he did useful chores, and in this work he gradually learned all the skills that were his father's.

And nothing more, for of what use would it have been to know anything else? And who could have taught him in any event? Tied to an economy of marginal productivity at best, he was reared purely to be the continuer of that economy; for him, the world of his father and his father's father was the only one conceivable, and with his training it would have been too much to expect that he would have readily accepted innovation and technological improvement even when told that such change would materially improve his lot. To have done so would have been to deny his forebears and all the assumptions on which his very existence depended. Little wonder, then, that medieval peasants should have proved initially so resistant to those very developments that were, in the end, to transform their lives.

To the modern mind the conditions endured by this peasantry inevitably appear appalling, for society at least since the Enlightenment has been built on the assumption that man can master his environment, producing a material progress that will lead to his own betterment. The spectre of a world not only ensnared in grinding poverty but, worse yet, actually resigned to it challenges our every belief about the nature of life. Although the twentieth century has seen more than its share of famine, cruelty and human degradation, we have coped with the horror by assuring ourselves that it is an aberration, a deviation from the norm. And even those who fear that such outcroppings of bestiality may be inherent in man, usually lurking beneath the surface but ever ready to burst forth when opportunity beckons, are nevertheless able to tell themselves that such things can always be controlled by proper manipulation and regulation of society's basic mechanisms.

To the medieval peasant, however, the world was a very different place. His whole outlook and upbringing had accustomed him to believe that his was the only possible life, and even though he might himself be more than half-starving, he could not conceive of a different one. This attitude involves something more – or less – than simple resignation. When one is resigned to one's fate, it is because one feels that nothing can be done about it. But few peasants ever rose to this level of consciousness, one which might allow them to entertain the possibility of different conditions. As a result, what to modern eyes looks like resignation was not really part of their character. Rather, they lived so intensely and concretely in the world as they found it that such thoughts could hardly have been expected to enter their heads.

With low population, scattered settlements, and impenetrable forests, Europe was not a place which easily gave rise to the notion that man was

the master of his environment. On the contrary, the immensity of an untamed nature made it appear that people, far from controlling the world
around them, were in fact held in thrall by it. For the peasant, life was lived
out in a primitive, one-room hovel. It could be variously constructed – of
rough wood, wattle and daub, sod or sun-baked bricks – but in no case did
it offer many creature comforts. With earthen floor, no windows, and a simple
hole in the thatched roof through which most of the smoke from the cooking
fire could pass, such homes provided only the barest protection from the
onslaught of the elements. Children, parents, and even grandparents were
crowded into the confines of these one-room structures, and not infrequently
they were joined by those few animals as the family might possess, particularly during the winter when the beasts, despite their obvious shortcomings
as cohabitants, did have the virtue of providing a warmth that would otherwise have been lacking.

The amenities were few. The beds (and often there was but one, shared by
all) were generally no more than piles of hay or straw that were seldom
replaced or renewed from one month to the next: such things were much
too valuable as forage to be wasted on human comfort. A table and possibly a
stool or two might occupy a corner, but little else graced the home other
than the implements of farm and domestic toil. In the centre burned the
fire, kindled on a circle of rocks, and over it hung the few earthenware cooking pots that also doubled as the serving dishes from which the family
communally ate its food.

Needless to say, these arrangements did little to foster a sense of indi-
viduality and privacy. All those acts and events that a prudish middle-class
culture tries to keep discreetly hidden took place in the sight of all. The
reticence and shame with which the modern world has frequently surrounded the everyday functions of birth, death, and love-making were feelings unknown in the medieval breast since there was no possible way in
which they could be shunted aside and veiled from the gaze of others. Indeed, it would be difficult to think of any other age in which the facts of life
came closer to being no more than just that.

Nevertheless, even though family relationships were intimate and close
(without being necessarily cordial), those with the surrounding community
could be much more ambiguous. On the one hand, because land tended to
be cultivated in a common field rather than in separate plots, all peasant
families in a hamlet found themselves tossed in each with the other, a
situation that was further encouraged by the fact that any individual's land
was apt to be scattered in strips throughout the common field. Further, since
few peasants could afford a plough or a full team of oxen, and since even
fewer had enough land to justify such possessions, each family tended to own
only part of a team and part of the equipment needed: as a result, close
co-operation had to develop if each was to get his work done. Similarly, the

very fact that most farming took place in one open field meant that the community had to agree on the dates when the field would be ploughed, harvested, turned over to gleaners, and, finally, opened to the cattle for forage.

In short, many aspects of the organization of a peasant hamlet led to the creation of feelings of intimacy. There were, however, a number of unpredictable variables. Most villages found themselves organized as manors under the control of a feudal lord, and in many instances the kinds of decisions that were elsewhere made by the peasants themselves were simply imposed by the arbitrary will of the lord or his steward, thus undercutting any sense of co-operation except in so far as this imposition from above fostered a sense, in some instances, of joint opposition. Then too, the physical layout of a village had much to do with the nature of the relationships that could be expected to exist within it. For farming communities were of two varieties, nuclear and dispersed. In the former, the dwellings of peasant and lord, not to mention barns, church, smithy and other buildings, were clustered tightly together, not unlike the typical small town of today. But in the latter there was no discernible nucleus; instead, homes were scattered widely over the countryside, with each family living as close as possible to the land it actually tilled.

No one knows precisely why these two different forms of villages should have arisen: some insist that they reflect the ethnic backgrounds of their inhabitants while others believe that the decision depended on the relative availability of water, the argument being that one central well led to a nuclear layout while a multiplicity of springs or a river encouraged dispersion. Yet, whatever the explanation, it is apparent that these two arrangements led to very different kinds of life. In the nuclear village, mutual intercourse arose naturally as all went to their toil in the fields together, as the women chatted with each other while doing their domestic tasks out of doors, and as families casually encountered one another on the streets. In a dispersed hamlet, on the other hand, these unexpected neighbourly meetings could take place much less easily and families had to rely much more on their own resources.

In either situation little opportunity arose for purely social encounters. To live was to work, and there was little enough time in a day to provide even for that. Inevitably, many activities in the agricultural year required the help of the whole community, for the rounding up of the half-wild pigs in the forest, the threshing of grain, and the construction of large projects such as a village barn could not be undertaken unless all were prepared to do their bit. Undoubtedly these joint labours had their social and relaxing aspects, probably not that much different from the so-called spinning and husking bees that did so much to relieve the monotony of life on the prairies of nineteenth-century America. Nevertheless, there was little else that could be called entertainment except on those rare occasions, great religious festivals like Christmas and Easter, when the community felt justified in setting a little time aside so that it might escape from its cares and give thanks to the Lord for its blessings.

This was, then, a relatively lonely existence. Family there might be in profusion, and a village community which interacted for its own survival. Yet the total number of people involved scarcely ever rose above a few hundred, and knowledge of the world seldom stretched in any concrete way beyond the limits of the manor and a few neighbouring hamlets.

Because the tenth and early eleventh centuries were an illiterate age, with a populace largely tied to the soil by law and tradition, the consequences were incalculable. Raised in one place, never having the opportunity or even the desire to travel, the peasant came to know his surroundings in ways unimaginable to men brought up in a world of urbanization and movement. Every detail of his physical surroundings was absorbed – the slope of each hillock, the place of each tree – and few activities of any individual or group did not immediately become the common knowledge of the whole community.

But news of the outside world arrived only intermittently and in distorted forms. The occasional traveller might bring word of happenings in far-distant lands, rumours of the doings of kings and princes, but little of this had meaning for the tiller of the soil. He knew nothing of geography, and that out there somewhere beyond the horizon there might be people and places pursuing lives totally different from his own must have struck him much as a romance or fairy tale strikes the young today – terribly exciting, enchanting, and entertaining, but not really to be believed. For the mentality of the peasant was not without its childlike aspects. Most striking, perhaps – at least in this context – are the curious time distortions that pervade the world of peasant and child alike. On the one hand, time in their daily lives is immediate and real, an inevitable progression of tasks and diversions that both stomach and sun can measure. Yet to move beyond that which is immediately and personally experienced is to enter a different reality, one in which all normal chronological assumptions disappear. In the evening, for example, the child lies in his bed and hears his mother begin: 'Once upon a time there was a beautiful princess named Rowena.' Suddenly, as he hears this, he is transported to another world, not of make-believe precisely, for he is perfectly prepared to accept Rowena's existence, but more one whose reality cannot be placed in any meaningful relationship to his own.

So too it was with the peasant. What he heard of lands beyond the manor took on the magical, enchanted properties of the world of 'once upon a time'. What pope or king did had no impact on him, and the events he heard related might have happened, for all he knew, two months ago, three years ago, or never at all. There was no way to find out, and, besides, like the child he could find few reasons for even wanting to. For the fact of the matter is that men at the millennium had little interest in, or understanding of, time

Agricultural Toil

Manorial life entailed many repetitive tasks such as the slaughter of pigs (*above*) and the tending of oxen (*below*).

Up to the millennium, beasts of burden were poorly yoked and ploughs consisted of little more than sharpened pieces of wood that scarcely scratched the soil. But in the eleventh century improved technology led to wheeled ploughs, harrows, and more efficient harnesses and yokes (*immediately below*). Blacksmiths increased – to provide shoes for horses and to make new implements (*bottom*).

Ploughing and seeding, from the *Très Belles Heures du duc de Berri*. To the nobility, manorial life often seemed idyllic.

In reality, the lot of
the common people
was harsh and barely
endurable: a German
serf, Mainz Cathedral.

and chronology as we conceive them today. By and large they were ignorant of dates and dating; seldom did they know even the length of their lives. Such things were irrelevant. What counted were simply sun and season, the progressions from solstice to solstice which so largely governed the ever-changing nature of their activities.

Here again one is struck by the extent to which men, far from being the masters of their environment, became its prisoners. People in the modern world approach each day knowing that it will have twenty-four hours of equal length, no matter what the season. About this there can be no doubt, for the unit of measurement is of human invention and can be successfully imposed day after day despite seasonal differences in the proportion of day-light to night-time hours. Nor do the duration and character of work neces-sarily change from summer to winter, for with artificial illumination and central heating men have learned to overcome the restrictions that an ever-varying natural order might otherwise place on his labours.

How different the life and experience of the medieval peasant. Everything was governed by the course of the sun. Men got up with its rising and retired at its setting, and if they were aware that this meant a working day hours longer in the summer, it was accepted as part of the divine and inscrutable plan for the universe. Similarly, the seasons dictated the work to be done, and the very success of that work depended not so much on the skill with which it was performed as on natural forces beyond men's control. If the crop failed, the peasant was not to blame; rather, it failed because the rain refused to fall or came in too great profusion, because winter lasted too long or came too early, because blight infested the fields or locusts descended upon them. Men could but labour and hope for the best.

Though few in number, the records of the age enable us to speak with some confidence about its view of the world and of elements moulding it. Little wonder, for example, that the peasantry – hemmed in, cut off, forced to accept whatever soil and weather would give them – should have endowed their physical surroundings with qualities of superstitious awe and fear. The forest might be the place where pigs could root and where berries, acorns and honey might be gathered, but it was also dark and impenetrable, inhospitable to man, the home of wild and ferocious beasts. In short, the forest was to be feared, and with an intensity and irrationality that escape our best attempts to capture them. Something of its terror lives on, perhaps, in the folk stories collected by the brothers Grimm, but even as we tremble with Hansel and Gretel or shudder at the sight of some distant and half-demonic charcoal burner, how can we even begin to appreciate the emotions of people for whom such a world was real, immediate, and all-too-visible beyond the last cultivated furrow?

Moreover, so little did man control his surroundings that all nature seemed to take on supernatural powers. Because no peasant could hope to comprehend the forces that shaped his life, he tended to endow them with animistic qualities and to assume that the world was governed by a host of capricious spirits which it lay beyond men's ability to understand, but whose future actions might be foreseen through portents. Even though religion insisted that the universe was God's creation, in their daily lives men seldom perceived it as a unified whole, interrelated and governed by a universal and rational order. On the contrary, they acted more on the belief that each aspect of nature was an entity unto itself, unpredictable, and usually hostile to the human condition. Or, more irrational yet, they assumed that unknown alliances might bind disparate elements together, and hence that human activities in one sphere of endeavour might bring wholly unexpected results, usually malign, in another.

Again, these beliefs and assumptions resemble nothing so much as those of the child, whose proverbs and nursery rhymes reflect a world equally at odds with modern knowledge. It is not reasonable to the adult, for example, to suppose that stepping on a crack will break his mother's back, but many are the children who upon occasion can believe in such sayings with an intensity that defies description. Similarly, in *Mother Goose* one can find rhymes whose outlook seem to go back to the millennium and to a people whose chance observations and discoveries could frequently be taken as portents of past, present and future:

> A swarm of bees in May
> Is worth a load of hay;
> A swarm of bees in June
> Is worth a silver spoon;
> A swarm of bees in July
> Is not worth a fly.

Then there are the charms and magical rites through which the hopeful can attempt to change their fate:

> The fair maid who, the first of May,
> Goes to the fields at break of day,
> And washes in dew from the hawthorn-tree,
> Will ever after handsome be.

In the twentieth century these jingles are no more than diversions for children, but a thousand years ago they or poems like them gave expression to a viewpoint shared by all ages and generations. This analogy with children is not meant to suggest that the medieval peasantry lived in a world of fairy-tale enchantment and romance similar to that of the child. After all, this view has never been a very accurate assessment of the experience of children, whose lives are all too often filled with the terrors of facing the unknown prospect of growing up, and if it is wrong with regard to children, there is even less reason to suppose that it applies with any justice to the lot of the medieval peasant.

For him, enchantment might well lie in the woods and fields surrounding his home, but it was hardly an enchantment in which men could take comfort and delight. Rather, it was to be feared as the malevolent spirit of an untamed nature. And what romance could be found in a world where most babies died young, where the starving ate grass, and where women could be yoked to the plough to replace the animal losses of winter? Europe around the year 1000 was no place for the weak and tender-hearted. Indeed, we can well ask whether it was a place for any kind of human existence at all.

2 The Feudal Aristocracy

Although it was the lot of peasants to work the land, even in the best of years they scarcely benefited from their labours. For the land was not theirs, but belonged to the feudal aristocracy, a group whose primary interest in agriculture lay in trying to squeeze the greatest possible revenue from the soil. The lord of a manor was little concerned with the misery of his tenants; that was their problem, and as long as rents continued to be paid and services performed, he saw little necessity for enquiring into living conditions and even less for doing anything about them. His efforts were instead dedicated to depriving the peasantry of all but the barest margin of survival.

It would be easy enough to ascribe this manorial oppression to nothing more than brutal rapacity and unthinking greed, but to do so would be to overlook the extent to which a marginal economy made such a situation almost inevitable. Brutal and unthinking as many lords undoubtedly were, their harshness and severity arose as much from circumstance as from choice. The aristocracy (it is still too early at the millennium to call it a nobility) claimed to be a governing elite; as such, it had to be free from the obligation of everyday toil. Yet, given the low level of agricultural productivity, no one could hope to escape from the life of the plough unless he could somehow force the rest of the community to reduce its already low standard of living in order to produce an artificial surplus on which he might live. That, precisely, was the function of manorialism, a system that squeezed and oppressed ninety-five per cent of the population so that the remaining five per cent could do something other than farm. We may not like manorialism, but before condemning it on humanitarian grounds we might remember that it alone made possible the fragmentary survival of government, church, and culture during some of Europe's darkest hours.

The techniques of manorialism were simple, but none the less effective. In return for the right to farm, peasants found themselves saddled with a host of obligations. A high proportion of the crop went to the lord as rent; two or three days a week were spent cultivating his land, and to his exclusive benefit; labour services were frequently expected for cartage, maintenance and anything else that struck the lord's fancy. And, as if these burdens were not enough, incidental payments were required at every turn: possibly a dozen eggs at Christmas, a piece of cloth at Easter, a plump goose at Midsummer, or a pig at All Souls – the list could be continued indefinitely.

Few people today are much concerned with the Seven Deadly Sins, but if they were, they might be struck by the inclusion of gluttony among them. Distasteful as over-indulgence may be, to modern eyes it hardly seems a vice worthy of such opprobrium. In the Middle Ages, however, and especially in the period preceding the advent of a relatively efficient agricultural system, this attitude was understandable. In a world pervaded by the threat of starvation, the contrast between the want of the peasantry and the affluence of the aristocracy must have appeared as an abomination in the sight of God, for how could He have been expected ever to accept or forgive the gluttony of the few, who could so callously stuff their bellies while allowing the many to waste away in misery and deprivation? No better commentary exists on medieval manners and morals than that gluttony should have become one of the Seven Deadly Sins, and that it did should certainly put to rest all romantic notions of a happy peasantry benignly ruled by a wise and considerate aristocracy.

We might expect that the inequities of manorialism would have led to constant social unrest, if not outright rebellion and revolution. Yet the fact of the matter is that peasant uprisings appear to have been relatively infrequent before the fourteenth century. In part this placidity arose from the tradition-directedness of the peasantry; that a better life could be created seemed inconceivable except in life after death, and in so far as any longing for it was confined to the religious sphere of expression, it scarcely threatened the aristocracy with a challenge to its position. Moreover, the magnitude of seigneurial authority provided a strong stabilizing influence. As a governing class, the aristocracy could bring to bear much more authority than that possessed by any modern landlord, and it is impossible to see how any peasant could have for long hoped to free himself from the all-embracing control of his lord. The aristocracy had a monopoly on arms and military training; increasingly it possessed primitive castles, difficult to storm; and it provided the laws and judicial system beyond which there was no appeal.

All of which placed the lord of a manor in a position of incredible strength. In effect, he combined his control of the land with his right to govern, thus creating a situation from which there was no escape. The vast majority of the peasantry were made into serfs, bound to the land and legally unfree, a class of men forbidden to leave the manor, prevented from marriage without formal and costly seigneurial permission, and incapable of owning property. Nor did the lord hesitate to use public authority (his so-called 'ban' power) to private ends since he, like the Merovingians before him, could see no difference between them. At his command, serfs built ovens and mills, signeurial monopolies that all on the manor were required to use, and, if there was recalcitrance, the lord or his steward would quickly mete out the appropriate punishment in the manorial court.

Needless to say, these circumstances have much to do with the formation of condescending attitudes toward those unfortunate enough not to have been born into the aristocracy. For much of the Middle Ages, at least down to the year 1000, lay society knew but two classes of men, increasingly differentiated – those who fought and those who toiled – and since only the oppression of the toilers made possible the ferocious activities of the fighters, the latter tended quite naturally to scorn those whose weakness, servility, and total lack of manliness both led to their degradation and prevented them from taking part in those martial pursuits on which alone claims to manhood and worth could be based. Doubtless there was in all this an element of unconscious rationalization, an attempt to justify the unjustifiable, but that did not make the scorn or disdain any less real.

Nevertheless, strong as was the position of the aristocracy with regard to the peasantry, its overall circumstances were far from enviable. On the continent, and particularly in northern France, most central authority had broken down during the ninth century under the impact of barbarian invasion and civil war. Counts in one region could expect no help from another, and in the absence of any outside constraints, they simply usurped what authority they could and began to claim it as a heritable right. In so doing, the counts almost never renounced their oaths of homage and fealty to the king, but even though these ties were retained, they rapidly ceased to have any practical significance. During these struggles counts were simultaneously attempting to increase their own powers by putting pressure on those in their counties weaker than themselves, forcing them to pledge homage, fealty and, above all, military assistance in times of need. Yet this proved a difficult task, for conditions not infrequently made it impossible for a count successfully to exert his control. It was easy enough for him to convince the defenceless – those people, for example, whose holdings lay unprotected and open to attack on a plain. But it was a different matter when he tried to cajole those whose resources equalled his own or whose lands were readily defended, as in a valley; such men might escape his control altogether.

Indeed, the pressures tending toward fragmentation were enormous. Just as the counts fought to break free from the authority of the king, those under them were equally determined to assert their own independence. Like Hobbes' state of nature, Europe in the ninth and tenth centuries found itself immersed in a struggle of each against all, and the irony of the situation was that most attempts to remedy matters only served to make them worse.

Counts soon discovered that in these turbulent times their counties were too large for one man to govern, so they were quick to appoint deputies, viscounts, who might share with them the burdens of defence and administration. In turn, the viscounts simply usurped from counts what they had initially usurped from the king. Then, in the tenth century, men developed what they hoped might prove a perfect solution: castles. Not only did they provide a strongpoint for defence; they could also serve as a bastion from which authority could be imposed on the surrounding countryside. If a count could build and man enough of them, he might yet be enabled to re-establish control.

Perhaps needless to say, these hopes were mistaken. With castles built and castellans installed to govern them, counts rapidly found that these men responded no more willingly to their commands than had the viscounts before them. A count could not be everywhere at once, but if he did not visit each castle with some frequency, his castellans soon forgot (if they had ever fully understood) that their powers were held only by virtue of delegation. Though counts kept endlessly to the saddle in a desperate effort to maintain lines of authority, many were to find that their claims to rule were honoured increasingly in the breach as castellans and viscounts revolted while others, with no such delegated titles of legitimacy, simply went their own way, erecting their own castles, thus further complicating an impossible situation.

As a charter once cited by Marc Bloch put it, the ninth and tenth centuries were a time when any ambitious man 'took possession of the land according to his power'.[20] By the millennium counties in many parts of Europe had ceased to exist as viable units of government; with notable exceptions like England, Flanders and Normandy, the true centres of power had devolved on the castellanies, and that this state of affairs was generally recognized is suggested by the few documents of the age, the vast majority of which refer to their point of origin in term of castellanies rather than counties, contrary to earlier practice. Although centralized authority would gradually reappear in the course of the next three centuries, few would have thought it likely around the year 1000.

While in school, students invariably learn of the feudal pyramid, that nice, well-ordered chain of command through which the king passed down his orders even to the lowliest vassal in the realm. Such a scheme, after all, makes for clear diagrams, and schoolboys have to begin somewhere. Nevertheless, where they do begin is rather far removed from reality. The tenth and early eleventh centuries knew no feudal pyramid, only a vicious power struggle in which all the bonds of society seemed dangerously close to dissolution. Oaths of homage and fealty continued to link most members of the aristocracy, but there was little hierarchy or chain of command. Few vassals felt constrained by these oaths to obey their lords, and although homage and fealty probably did something to prevent direct and murderous attacks on those to whom they had been sworn, they in no way hindered the greedy from seizing rights, property and authority when opportunity beckoned.

Some historians have referred to these conditions as 'feudal anarchy', but

47

the phrase is misleading, at least from the point of view of the participants. In modern terms, any political system devoid of authority is *ipso facto* anarchic; to the medieval mind, however, much of the chaos derived from a scrupulous concern for law, justice and order, qualities that are not usually associated with anarchy. This difference in interpretation arises from contrary notions of justice and law, for whereas the modern world conceives of them as emanations of the state, positive decisions and enactments created and enforced by the will of men, the Middle Ages had another view. Law was God's law: eternal, immutable, and totally removed from any human power to change or amend. Man's role was limited strictly to discovering that law, something that could best be done by searching out the precedents of the past. In practical terms, then, law was custom, and justice was no more than the observance of the law.

When applied, these theories led to unexpected results, largely because of the peculiar circumstances in which the aristocracy found itself. Like the peasants, the typical lord was illiterate and, having no records to speak of, his memory of the past was both imprecise and of limited extent. Moreover, greed and ambition can do curious things to the mind, convincing it time and time again that precedents exist which can justify even the most selfish of actions. And if they do, then those actions, far from being selfish, become wholly legal, proper, and necessary. Because law was discovered and not made, it became intensely personal, the property of its discoverer and not easily subject to impartial review. In a sense, law existed only in the mind of each individual and, thanks to the intellectual characteristics of the times, a man could rapidly change his views on the nature of legality without even realizing it. 'Dieu et mon droit' may now be thought of as nothing more than a motto on the British coat of arms, but for much of the Middle Ages it could have been used by any member of the aristocracy, each one of whom was prepared to defend God and his own right.

When viewed in this light, 'feudal anarchy' takes on rather different colours. The viscount or castellan may have been rapacious and greedy in throwing off the count's authority, and yet in so doing both undoubtedly believed that they had law and justice on their side. In all likelihood neither one saw much of the count after he had assigned them their duties, and over the years each grew accustomed to making his own decisions, free from any external interference. In the same way, most found it relatively easy to pass their posts on to their sons. Not surprisingly, then, they were outraged on those rare occasions when the count chose to reassert his authority, since from their point of view the count's actions appeared uncustomary and therefore illegal. Such disagreements led inevitably to war and possibly to anarchy, but the real point is that the ensuing chaos derived from a curious adherence to legality rather than from any conscious desire to overthrow the principles on which society had been founded.

What is apparent, however, is that this period saw the origins of the tendency, so notable later in Europe, to think of the aristocracy as a self-justifying law unto itself. Effectively removed from the control of any superior, and regarding justice as nothing more than observance of those precedents remembered from the past, the aristocracy of the millennium began to develop an outlook hostile to any attempts aimed at subjecting it to outside authority, either moral or legal. Since law was so largely self-generated, no lord could possibly admit that others had a right to limit and restrain his conduct. To have done so would have been to deny all those assumptions that gave meaning to his world.

Nowhere is this attitude more evident than in the private wars and trials by combat that were so characteristic of the age. Even if a state had existed, no matter how powerful, it could not easily have imposed its jurisdiction on the squabbles of the aristocracy, for they originated in quarrels about a law which God, not the state, had established, a law that each individual had to discover for himself and that was not to be found in any legislation enacted by man. To satisfy the demands of that law, each lord had necessarily to be judge in his own case since he alone knew where justice lay, and in the absence of any other possibility for enforcement, he was forced to appeal to God and to a trial by arms in which the divine mercy would surely decide for the right. Only in this way could honour and the obligations of 'Dieu et mon droit' be properly satisfied, and that this attitude of mind was no mere passing fancy is suggested by the prevalence of duelling right down to the nineteenth century. Despite the state's best efforts to eradicate it, the nobility would not readily give up this last form of a trial by combat that carried with it distant memories of an age in which the aristocracy was accountable not to mortal men, but solely to God.

So the lord of the year 1000 fought and fought frequently. The possibilities for altercation were endless: disputed boundaries, personal affronts, uncertain rights and obligations – such questions and more were ever present as causes for an appeal to arms. As a result, the aristocracy of the period never became a true nobility, a closed caste limited to those lucky enough to be born into it. On the contrary, it remained open to those whose cunning, prowess and luck enabled them to wrest land and authority from those who, for whatever reason, proved incapable of resisting. Others entered the ruling élite more purely by chance. In France, for example, knights had traditionally been no more than mounted warriors, fighters whose other attributes in no way qualified them as members of the governing class. From the mid-tenth century on, however, the king and other territorial lords found it increasingly difficult to attract important vassals to their courts even on those great feast days when all men were expected to rally around their lords so that the latter could the better display their magnificence and power. Faced with this recalcitrance and unable to cope with it, king and counts alike began to

D

summon knights to fill the ranks, and as knights appeared, they soon found themselves burdened with the rudimentary legal and administrative duties that had formerly been the exclusive prerogative of those much above them in station. As a result, knighthood began to flower for the first time, gaining recognition as a natural and normal element in the ruling aristocracy.

Because the aristocracy lived in a world of social fluidity bordering on legalized chaos, the quest for security became of primary concern. Here two distinct alternatives presented themselves, reliance on family and reliance on feudalism. One could look to the family for protection, hoping that a shared blood would lead relatives to support each other in times of danger, or one could turn to the feudal bond, hoping that homage and fealty would create a network of mutual obligations sufficient to provide for common security.

In practice, of course, these choices were seldom mutually exclusive. Help was where you found it, and the lord who saw himself hard-pressed by a host of troubles was likely to appeal both to family and vassals for aid. Nevertheless, such an appeal often proved the source of increased tension and hostility, for family obligations and feudal obligations were seldom harmonious. Thus a man under attack might find that his cousins, his last hope of salvation, were vassals of those attacking him, and to ask them for aid was to place them in an impossible position. Indeed, so common does this problem seem to have been – and so troubling – that it was to become one of the great themes of the feudal epics when the aristocracy began to find a literary voice toward the end of the eleventh century.

Nowhere is the theme more starkly presented than in *Raoul de Cambrai*, a late twelfth-century *chanson de geste* whose hero we have already encountered fasting for Lent after burning a convent. At the opening of the tale Raoul is even before birth wrongfully dispossessed of his rightful inheritance, the Cambrésis. Upon gaining his maturity, he demands of the king that he be given the fief of the next lord to die, who turns out to be Herbert de Vermandois. Unfortunately, however, Herbert has left four sons, all prepared to defend their lands, and the situation is further complicated by the fact that Bernier, Herbert's grandson, has become Raoul's squire. All this notwithstanding, with the king's consent Raoul determines to conquer the Vermandois and to claim it as his own. Raoul's own disinheritance is thus to be remedied by the disinheritance of his squire.

Without dwelling on the details of the ensuing conflict, it is apparent that Bernier has been ensnared by the family-feudal dilemma. Bound by oath to serve Raoul, his services can only further the agonies of his family. Yet loyal to Raoul he remains, and the question soon becomes how far his lord will be able to push him before he will renounce his allegiance and go to the aid of his father and uncles. Raoul devastates the countryside and even murders his squire's mother (one of the nuns consumed in the convent fire at Origny) without Bernier's lifting a finger against him. Only when he strikes his squire in anger with the butt end of a lance does Bernier feel free to hurl his defiance and to join his father's avenging army.

Rude and barbaric as *Raoul de Cambrai* may now appear, it is a tale that spoke to the condition of its audience. In suggesting through Bernier that the bonds of feudalism should take precedence over those of the family, it was probably arguing for the world as it ought to be, not as it was, but in its acceptance of Bernier's right to break the ties of homage and fealty after personal affront, it was surely in accord with the mood of the times. The self and its honour came naturally to the fore, and it followed logically from this that if they were attacked or impugned, all else had to be subordinated to their defence. Indeed, when viewed in this light even the outrageous Raoul takes on a certain unexpected dignity, for his actions all sprang from an understandable need to blot out the dishonour visited upon him by his exclusion from the rightful succession to the Cambrésis. Totally justified in motive, Raoul met tragedy by being unable to see that his own course of action in attacking the Vermandois would inevitably lead to the dishonouring of others, thus bringing about his own doom.

Similar themes lie at the heart of *The Song of Roland,* the most familiar of the twelfth-century *chansons.* Like *Raoul de Cambrai,* it occasionally reflects interests untypical of the millennium (notably its emphasis on a crusading ethic), but more than *Raoul* it introduces the reader to the full range and complexity of feudal values as they were shared by the vast majority of the aristocracy around the year 1000. To come to grips with *The Song of Roland* is to encounter in vivid detail all those problems and conflicts to which no amount of generalization can give immediacy and life.

The plot itself is familiar. For seven years Charlemagne has been attempting to conquer and convert the Paynims of Spain, and at this point Roland suggests that Ganelon be sent to parley with Marsila, the Paynim king. Furious, and hating Roland for suggesting this dangerous mission, Ganelon decides to plot with Marsila, who then treacherously promises Charlemagne that he will become a Christian if the Franks will retire from Spain. The Frankish leader agrees, and at Ganelon's insistence Roland is appointed captain of the rear guard which, while wending its way through the vale of Ronceval, is suddenly attacked and slaughtered despite heroic resistance that leads in the end to symbolic victory. In a trial by combat Ganelon is found guilty of treason and is sentenced to be torn limb from limb by four swift stallions. Justice is served, and so ends the oldest known version of the epic.

Although this tale is simple enough in outline, its details offer surprising insights into the mentality of the times. Here, for example, is a story involving Charlemagne, heroic 'lord of the land of France', and that he was truly a figure of awe there can be no doubt:

51

> In the shade
> Of a tall tree, beside an eglantine,
> Uprose a throne of purest gold, and there
> The great King sat who held sweet France in sway.
> White was his beard and all snow-white his hair,
> In face and form the noblest of them all.
> If any man would find the King, there needs
> No guide.[21]

Yet this great king is strikingly incapable of independent action. Again and again, when confronted with a decision, he remains silent, unable to act, until he has taken counsel with the wisest of his knights; only after they have spoken and arrived at general agreement does he speak, and then always simply to ratify the decision of his vassals. In short, the Charlemagne of *The Song of Roland* is an ideal monarch for an aristocracy whose chief aim for centuries had been to escape the domination of superior authority by establishing its own claims to power. And that the greatness of Charlemagne rests ultimately on the abilities of his vassals there can be no doubt; as Roland puts the case at the beginning of the second battle:

> 'The men who fight this fight are good
> And true. There is no king in the wide world
> Has better men, and therefore is it writ
> In Frankish story that our King is great.'[22]

The king's actions, then, depend on his men, and for them the concept of 'honour' plays a crucial role. Thus, when Roland proposes Ganelon for the embassy to Marsila and the Franks agree, Ganelon can only accept, angry as he is, for to do otherwise would be to risk a suggestion of cowardice. Indeed, his honour is badly tarnished when he drops the gauntlet given to him by Charlemagne as a symbol of his embassy. Similarly, although no one concurs and the king positively objects when Ganelon suggests that Roland head the rear guard, Roland nevertheless gets the appointment by making his selection a matter of honour:

> And Roland said: 'O King, give me the curving bow
> Thou holdest – ay – and by that token give
> The rear guard to me. None shall say – methinks –
> I let it fall, as Ganelon let fall
> Your glove.' But the King wept, and sat a time
> In troubled thought, and fingered his white beard.

> Then stood forth Naimon, oldest of the Franks,
> And wisest, saying: 'You have heard, O King,
> The angry words of Roland. There is none
> May claim the rear guard now. Give him your bow,
> And choose good men to aid him.' And the King,
> Shuddering, laid the bow in Roland's hand.[23]

In the course of the epic, however, the concept of honour becomes increasingly complex as its preservation is seen to involve not only the upholding of the dignity of self (as in the case of Roland above), but also the proper observance of family and feudal obligations. When Oliver repeatedly asks Roland to summon Charlemagne's aid by blowing his horn, the complexities of honour are wonderfully demonstrated in the variety of Roland's refusals:

> 'Friend, I were mad to heed you. I should lose
> The praise of men forever in sweet France.
> Nay, I shall draw my sword, and steep the blade
> In Paynim blood up to the hilt. . . .'

> 'God forfend!
> No living man shall say I winded horn
> For Paynims! Such indignity shall not
> Abase my kindred! . . .'

> 'God forbid
> That I bring low my kindred, or become
> The instrument of my dear land's dishonor. . . .'

> 'Friend, of this no more! for here
> In Ronceval are twenty thousand Franks,
> But not one coward. It is Frankish law
> That every man must suffer for liege lord
> Or good or ill, or fire or wintry blast,
> Ay, truly, must not reck of life or limb. . . .'[24]

Roland is not alone is this devotion to honour; it permeates the thinking of all the Franks. Even Ganelon sees his quest for vengeance as a defence of honour impugned, and once he has uttered his formal defiance and hatred of Roland, he must carry out his threats simply to preserve the integrity of his word. Dragged back to France in chains and accused of treason, he cannot even begin to comprehend the charges against him:

> 'For God's sweet love, hearken! my lords! The King
> Speaks truth, saying that I was in the host
> That conquered Spain, and him I served in faith
> And love. But Roland it was who sent me to the King
> Of Paynim Spain, and I living returned
> Through mine own cunning. True it is I took
> A swift and fearful vengeance, not alone
> On Roland, but on Oliver his friend,
> And all their comrades – lawful vengeance though,
> For had I not defied them? Charles the King
> Heard me, and heard me all his soldiers. Thus
> I paid them all – but treason it was not.'[25]

So personalized have all relations become that the traitor – and much of his audience – cannot grasp the fact that his dealings with Marsila and the subsequent slaughter at Ronceval had anything treasonous in them. Because Ganelon intended no harm to Charlemagne himself, he fails to see that any was done. Thus does the spirit of 'Dieu et mon droit' make Ganelon a loyal vassal in his own eyes to the end.

Yet *The Song of Roland* is more than a study of honour; above all else it is an epic of battle, a paean of praise to those who fight, for it is only in battle that men can rise to the fullness of their potential. Roland is great because he would rather fight than think; Archbishop Turpin is admired because: 'Never did priest sing mass, who with his hands/Did greater deeds in battle.'[26] And the standards are high. As the archbishop puts them:

> 'He who bears arms, and sits on a good steed
> Is thereby bounden to be brave and strong
> Though facing fearful odds. Stands he not firm,
> Nor fights with doubled strength, I should not give
> Two farthings for him. . . .'[27]

Everywhere there is an unconcealed delight in the violence of the fray, and nowhere more striking than when Roland himself is engaged:

> He drew his trenchant sword,
> His trusted Durendal, and spurred apace
> On the swart gnome who ruled the Hills of Darkness.
> Him did he smite, and the keen blade cut through
> The Paynim's helmet, through his matted hair,
> Down through his head and black, misshapen frame,
> Rending his hauberk like a rag, and through
> The golden saddle, slaying horse and man
> With one great blow.[28]

Such scenes could hardly fail to arouse the blood-lust of their hearers, and that the poet was well aware of their probable popularity is suggested by the frequency with which they appear. Valour, strength, brutality: all the aspects of a virile manliness are hymned, and often in a manner calculated to make the audience regret that it too had been unable to gain glory by death in the magnificent slaughter:

> So the Franks fought on,
> Though sore beset. Would you had seen the fight!
> Would you had seen Count Roland and his friend
> Smite with their swords! and with his pointed spear
> The good Archbishop! Thousands did they slay –
> So it is written in the Book of France –
> Four battles did they fight, and win – the fifth

Went not so well. Alas, of all the Franks
Sixty alone are left, whom God has spared
Till now – and dear will they sell their lives.[29]

Without doubt, fighting was the stuff of life. And little wonder, since from earliest youth the feudal aristocracy was trained for nothing else. For the lord of the year 1000, the world revolved around arms – around the use of sword, shield, mace and lance; around the proper fit of helm and chain-mail hauberk; around the breeding and selection of warhorses fit to bear armoured weight with speed and agility. Even in its diversions – wrestling, jousting and, above all, hunting – the aristocracy continued its training. No peasant could hunt; this sport was the preserve of their lords, and for understandable reasons. To track down a boar, to bring him to bay, and then to lay him low with arrow or spear was to gain in strength, courage, and martial skills, dangerous talents for peasants to possess. For the aristocracy, however, they were vitally needed.

Yet despite the surge of excitement that one inevitably feels while reading the great feudal epics, the modern reader is left with the sense that the typical lord of the age led a life that was essentially limited, boring, and sterile. Illiterate, crude, and totally lacking in emotional restraints, the aristocracy was a group whose only thoughts were of war and the battlefield. In its hands government disintegrated for want of interest and training; each man was content to seize what he could and manage it wholly to his own advantage. Honour was all, and with emotions so close to the surface, even petty or imagined slights led to endless private wars in which the only real losers were the peasants, whose fate it was to see their fields constantly trampled and burned by warriors whose code of honour was totally devoid of any concern for those less fortunate and powerful than they. Such an existence may have had its momentary attractions, especially for knights still in the vigour of youth, but it is difficult to believe that over the years it could have provided many men with much sense of gratification and fulfillment. Indeed, perhaps the saving grace of this life was that few lived long enough to experience its shortcomings.

Moreover, what was merely limiting for a lord became a positive desert for his wife. The world of the millennium was not yet that of courtly romance and of fair damsels placed on a pedestal of knightly devotion. On the contrary, this was a world in which women occupied a position little better than chattel. No lord married for love; rather, he married for wealth and security, for the landed dowry and family alliances that his wife could be expected to bring him. If he took any personal interest in the lady at all, it was purely in his concern that she come from good breeding stock so that the preservation of his lineage might be better assured.

By and large, women could own no property, and in all matters both great and small they were entirely subject to their husband's whim. And the castle of the late tenth and early eleventh centuries was not a particularly pleasant place to live: still of the so-called motte and bailey variety, it consisted of little more than a few rude buildings surrounded by a wooden palisade. Although more comfortable that the peasants' hovels, it was subject nonetheless to winter's icy blasts, and even the breezes of a bright summer day were apt to carry with them the stench of men and animals too long and too closely confined.

For better or worse, this was the woman's domain. Here she bore her children, not infrequently dying in the process. Here she awaited the return of husband and sons from battle, with what mixture of emotions it is impossible to say. Here, in short, she spent her days in an endlessly monotonous round of needlework, child-rearing, and supervision of domestic labours from which only death – or in widowhood the convent – could provide release.

For the aristocracy, then, life was far from being an earthly paradise. Even though it faced few of the horrors experienced by the peasantry, it had horrors enough of its own, ones separated from those of the peasants more by differences in degree than of kind. The truth is that torment and tragedy were the constant companions of rich and poor alike, and if it had not been for the powerful influence exerted on society by religion, it might seem incomprehensible that so few men rose up to curse and rebel against their fate. Once religion is taken into account, however, this passivity becomes more understandable. Imperfect as the Church of the age may have been, at least it assured the believer that the tearing physical reality of this life was no more than a way station on the road to that eternal Heavenly City from which all earthly cares would be banished. At times this message must have seemed a small consolation to those bereft, and yet, because it was all there was, men clung to it with passionate tenacity. And in that tenacity the primacy of the Church was established.

The Majesty of Kings

Medieval literature is filled with the theme of royal majesty betrayed: here Mark kisses his nephew Tristan before the fatal encounter with Iseult. A thirteenth-century tile found at Chertsey, England.

St Louis (*left*) succeeded with great simplicity in capturing the hearts of his subjects. No one prevailed against Charlemagne, the archetype of the warrior-king (*above*).

Harold was a real monarch undone (*above*), and Otto III (*below*) died unsuccessful and young, despite the majesty to which he aspired.

The Church claimed the power to make and unmake kings: here Archbishop Peter Aspelt of Mainz (*left*) crowns kings of the Holy Roman Empire. Monarchs like Edward the Confessor (*right*) were quick to do the Church's bidding.

3 The Church

For the very young, the world seems a place of unpredictable mystery, totally removed from the control of physical laws of cause and effect. All things appear possible, and that the child really believes this is nowhere better demonstrated than in his endless fascination with magic. He knows that he himself cannot produce flowers out of thin air or saw ladies in half, but having seen others perform these tricks, he rests confident in the assumption that they are real and that a growing maturity will confer on him the skills needed to duplicate them. In the meantime he practises, hopefully muttering: 'Hocus-pocus, dominocus' and 'Abracadabra, please and thank you' over playthings selected for disappearance or transformation. In so doing, he little realizes that he is sharing in an attitude of mind prevalent a thousand years ago.

Indeed, it may be that even the very vocabulary of these childish incantations goes back to the millennium. Certainly the words are of medieval invention, and in their origins they reflect something of the awe felt by an ignorant populace for the incomprehensible skills of the clergy. Although 'abracadabra' is itself meaningless, it derives from a simple recitation of the alphabet, and in this painful sounding out of 'a, b, c, d' one can possibly sense the wonder of the illiterate confronted with men who could find meaning and content on a page covered with nothing more than inky blotches and scratches. So great was this wonder, in fact, that many people came to believe that 'abracadabra', when written triangularly and worn on an amulet, provided a charm that would ward off disease.

Similarly, the nonsense sounds of 'hocus-pocus, dominocus' are an obvious imitation of the Latin of the mass, a language unknown by the laity and assumed by them to have magical properties. This assumption should not be surprising, for what could have been more miraculous than the priest's ability to change ordinary bread and wine into the living body and blood of Christ simply by intoning a few Latin phrases from the liturgy? Denied even the rudimentary education of most of the clergy, aristocracy and peasantry alike were quick to suppose that the miracle of the sacraments depended in no small measure on the magical qualities of the language in which they were performed. And from that belief it is but a small step to the child's faith in 'hocus-pocus'.

The real point, however, is not that children today rely on magical incantations developed in the Middle Ages; rather it is that medieval man lived in a culture so saturated by primitive superstition that he could scarcely imagine a world in which the miraculous did not play a predominant role. Moreover, the very nature of his everyday life led him desperately to search for a meaning to his existence that lay outside the harsh physical reality of his daily experience.

The borderline between superstition and religion is at best rather shadowy, but in general it can be said that superstition involves little more than a highly discrete set of hopes and fears about particular objects and practices whereas religion, especially in its higher forms, carries with it a whole range of relatively coherent doctrines that attempt to impart meaning to life. Medieval Christianity taught, for example, that God had created man, only to see him fall through his sin in the Garden, a sin transmitted to all his descendants who were thereby denied life everlasting and forced to earn their bread by the sweat of their brow. But God had taken pity on man, and in the Person of His only begotten Son He had become flesh and dwelt in the world of men. In His crucifixion He had taken on and atoned for the sins of the world, and in His resurrection He had guaranteed salvation and life everlasting to those who believed. And, lastly, on the rock that was Peter He had founded His Church, whose mission it was to spread and preserve the faith, thus making it possible for all men to be saved.

The theological complexities of this story are enormous, and it seems doubtful that even many of the clergy could begin to understand them at this time. Nevertheless, dimly as men perceived Christ's message and badly as they knew even the bare outlines of His story, Christianity developed a compelling appeal. It provided an explanation for earthly travail and, more than that, it offered hope that this life would be succeeded by another more perfect one in which the cares and tragedies of the world would be replaced by a blissful eternity in the sight of God.

For men caught in a web of circumstances in which peasants starved while the powerful plundered and brutalized each other, Christianity gave what little meaning there was to earthly existence. If life then was as terrifying as we have every right to believe, men must have been desperately anxious to escape their fate, to rise out of their wretched conditions in order to taste at least some of that peace and contentment once known by Adam. Yet there was no possibility of physical escape. Like it or not, men were doomed to a miserable estate, and much as they might struggle, these struggles served only to increase their misery by emphasizing it. On the other hand, insofar as Christianity taught that this life was but a preparation for the next, it held out hope for the future if only the believer would resign himself to present conditions.

Because religion offered the only balm available, men held to it fiercely. Moreover, the ignorance and illiteracy of the age intensified the faith, for the faith was the Church, and anyone could see that its priesthood possessed knowledge and miraculous powers shared by no others. In so saying, we return, perhaps, to the world of 'hocus-pocus' and superstition, but it was nevertheless one in which superstitious elements, even though flourishing in basically pagan and anti-Christian forms, were harnessed to the greater ends of the Church.

What emerges from a study of the documents is a picture of a religion both under pressure and making progress. For much of the population the peace of God passed all understanding and the Christian message had little effect on the way they conducted their daily lives. Still semi-pagan and conditioned to brutality, such people were not to be remade overnight into exemplars of Christian sainthood. Yet, despite all the violence and super- stition, there was a bedrock of belief: no matter how much men might cry out against their fate and attempt to escape it, they never thought to question their Maker or to blame Him for the wretchedness of their lives. In the end, then, there was a certain sense of resignation and humility pervading the world of the millennium, and in so far as this was the case, the Church had adequate materials on which to build.

This is not to say, however, that the Church was capable of building, for it, like the rest of society, had fallen on evil times. To those within the faith, the Church as an institution is the vessel of God's holy truth, infallible and unerring, but at the same time all would acknowledge that the Church on earth is made up of men, frail creatures subject to temptation and sin. Thus, although the institution itself may remain inviolate, its members – and even the highest among them – may stray like lost sheep far from the flock and the Shepherd who protects them. This can be true in any period, but at no time has it been more strikingly demonstrated than in the century and a half of chaos that rent the Church following the collapse of the Carolingian Empire.

By the end of the ninth century the papacy had become a prize fought over by contending factions in the Roman aristocracy. The violence and sacrilege were appalling. John VIII was the first pope to be murdered, in 882, but during the late ninth and tenth centuries many others were to follow: Stephen VI was strangled; Benedict VI was smothered; and John XIV was eliminated by unknown means in the papal residence of Castel Sant'Angelo. Even those deaths which could be considered natural not infrequently suggested a lack of spirituality, as witness Liutprand of Cremona's report that: 'One night when John [XII] was disporting himself with some man's wife outside Rome, the devil dealt him such a violent blow on the temples that he died of the injury within a week'.[30] This was hardly the way for a pope to go, and John's reputation was not further enhanced by the rumour, widely circulated in Rome, that to the end he had refused administration of the last sacraments of the Church.

Nor was there peace even in the grave. When Formosus died in 896, a rival faction seized power. Not content with its control of the papacy, this party had Formosus' corpse exhumed, clad in full pontifical regalia, placed on the chair of St Peter, and tried for immorality and heresy. Found guilty, the body was stripped and, after having the fingers of papal benediction hacked off, it was dragged naked through the streets of Rome and dumped in the Tiber.

In the first half of the tenth century it was the turn of the so-called house of Alberic to rule. Alberic's mother and grandmother, Marozia and Theodora, first established the family's claims to power, and gossip was quick to associate their names with those of a half-dozen popes either as mistress, mother or murderess. Alberic continued their tradition from 932 to 954, and after his death he was succeeded by a son who, no longer content simply to rule, had himself proclaimed pope as John XII in 955. He was eighteen at the time. Hardened as men were, the reign of John XII proved more than his contemporaries could stand. To Liutprand of Cremona John's manner of death was the least of his crimes, and the pages of Liutprand's *Liber de Rebus Gestis Ottonis* are filled with tales of John's misdeeds ranging from dicing and whoring to the murder by castration of one of his cardinals. But the good bishop should be allowed to speak for himself:

Pope John is the enemy of all [pure] things. What we say is a tale well known to all. As witness to its truth take the widow of Rainer his own vassal, a woman with whom John has been so blindly in love that he has made her governor of many cities and given to her the golden crosses and cups that are the sacred possessions of St. Peter himself. Witness also the case of Stephana, his father's mistress, who recently conceived a child by him and died of an effusion of blood. If all else were silent, the palace of the Lateran, that once sheltered saints and is now a harlot's brothel, will never forget his union with his father's wench, the sister of the other concubine Stephania. Witness again the absence of all women here save Romans: they fear to come and pray at the thresholds of the holy apostles, for they have heard how John a little time ago took women pilgrims by force to his bed, wives, widows and virgins alike. Witness the churches of the holy apostles, whose roof lets the rain in upon the sacrosanct altar, and that not in drops but in sheets. The woodwork fills us with alarm, when we go there to ask God's help. Death reigns within the building, and, though we have much to pray for, we are prevented from going there and soon shall be forced to abandon God's house altogether.[31]

In purveying these tales Liutprand was doubtless being little more than the gossip-monger. As a loyal follower of Otto I, refounder of the medieval Empire, he had small cause to like John, and many of the charges he brought were already becoming clichés in the rhetoric of papal abuse. On the other hand, it would be wrong to suppose that his picture of John was wholly lacking in foundations, for when Otto attempted to intervene in Rome, he quickly gained the support of those prelates whose purity of life had already brought them into open conflict with the pope. That such men were willing to accept secular power as their saviour from spiritual abuse certainly suggests that Liutprand's story, although overdrawn, still managed to convey the truth about John and conditions in Rome.

Conditions did not rapidly improve. Despite the interventions of Otto and subsequent emperors, the papacy remained largely the plaything of contending Roman factions. In the early eleventh century it fell into the hands of the counts of Tusculum who, from 1012 on, managed to elevate three members of their family in succession to the throne of St Peter: Benedict VIII, his brother John XIX, and their nephew Benedict IX.

Of these three, the nephew most deserves our attention. Becoming pope in 1032, Benedict IX was soon embroiled in the usual factional struggles. In 1044 the Crescentii seized power, drove Benedict from Rome, and in the following year installed their own papal candidate, Sylvester III. But Benedict and the Tusculan clan rallied their forces, and long before the end of 1045 the eternal city was again theirs. At this point, however, Benedict seemed rapidly to be tiring of his spiritual duties, so he announced, in effect, that he would auction off the papacy to the highest bidder even as the Praetorian Guard had sold the Roman Empire after the murder of Commodus.

The successful bidder turned out to be a wealthy but reform-minded archpriest who had apparently become so appalled by the scandalous state of affairs that he could see no remedy for the situation other than to play the game and, even at the risk of the sin of simony, to purchase the papal office so that it could at last be put to better purposes. Taking the name of Gregory VI, he had scarcely begun the task of restoration when Benedict IX suddenly went back on his bargain and proclaimed that he was once again resuming his duties.

In 1046, then, Rome confronted the world with the spectacle of three warring popes. Sylvester III still retained St Peter's and the Vatican; Benedict IX claimed the Lateran Palace; and Gregory VI began to fortify the basilica of Santa Maria Maggiore. Since each had supporters among the Roman mob, riots filled the streets and Rome was reduced to chaos. Only with the intervention of the German emperor, Henry III, was order restored: all three popes were deposed, and Henry's own nominee, Clement II, was elected to succeed them. With the elevation of Clement, genuine reform finally came to the papacy after a century and a half of violence and corruption.

To the modern reader, these degrading events conjure up little thought of the miraculous and magical usually associated with religion; on the contrary, the history of the papacy in the years preceding and following the millennium seems consciously calculated to revolt the sensibilities of the faithful. And to some extent, of course, that was the result: the more ardent were repelled, and to prove the point one has only to turn to the outraged pages of Liutprand of Cremona and to the writings of the growing number of reformers who were ultimately to prevail in the latter half of the eleventh century. Nevertheless, indignation and outrage are but half of the story.

No institution can ever rise above the standards set by its personnel, and in so far as these men inevitably reflect the values and mores of the age that gives them birth, all institutions tend to evolve with the times, blending into the background of society's changing assumptions in such a way that particular institutional strengths and weaknesses become hidden by the parallel strengths and weaknesses of the society itself. In a sense, nothing more is involved than a case of cultural 'boilerman's deafness', an inability to recognize defect or merit simply because of its all-pervasiveness.

It seems very apparent that in the tenth century the papacy's reputation benefited from the effects of such a phenomenon. As men grew accustomed to the sight of an aristocracy struggling to seize power from those supposedly in authority, many lost the ability to see anything morally perverse in the feuds and vendettas that surrounded the see of St Peter. Moreover, the difficulty of communications so characteristic of the age prevented much of the scandal from reaching a wider audience beyond the Alps. Finally, personalized though society had become, religion's appeal lay not in men, but rather in its ultimate meaning, a meaning symbolized in the miracle of the mass. For men with minds so attuned, Rome ceased to be a dirty, under-populated town on the Tiber, filled with intrigue and overflowing with savage corruption. It transcended the bloody actuality of its existence and became the Eternal City, a symbol of all that was best in imperial and papal tradition. Even under Alberic a poet could write:

> O Roma nobilis, orbis et domina,
> Cunctarum, urbium excellentissima,
> Roseo martyrum sanguine rubea,
> Albis et virginum liliis candida . . .
>
> [O noble Rome, mistress of the world,
> Of all earthly cities most excellent,
> Resplendent in red with the blood of the martyrs,
> Shining lily-white with the virtue of virgins . . .][32]

Yet, no matter what poets might hymn and others imagine, Rome was totally incapable of providing that spiritual leadership so desperately needed for the regeneration of religious life in the Church. As symbol, Rome continued to govern the world, but in practice she had lost control over all instruments of ecclesiastical rule. Drawn inward on herself and her own problems, torn apart by the savagery of personal and family ambitions, she no longer took an interest in the affairs of her bishops: like the counts of the fallen Carolingian Empire they were allowed to go their own ways, unfettered by any bonds of temporal or spiritual obedience. Rome had become a place of pilgrimage, nothing more.

Although free from the domination of Rome, few bishops had much cause for satisfaction. Everywhere in Europe those forces that had so utterly destroyed the political fabric of life proved equally destructive to the Church. In 909 a provincial synod at Reims reported:

Cities are depopulated, monasteries are in ruins and ashes, and the country is reduced to a wasteland. Every man does what pleases him, despising the laws of God and man and the ordinances of Holy Church. Some monasteries have been destroyed by the heathen, others despoiled of their lands. In those which have survived the monastic rule is no longer observed, and there are no longer any legitimate superiors, because of the domination of monasteries by lay abbots with their wives and children, and with their soldiers and dogs.[33]

Even after making due allowance for the hyperbole common to such statements, the picture presented is far from reassuring. Indeed, from a modern perspective conditions were in fact much more perniciously grave than those at the time appreciated. Spectators always see more of the game than the players, and in the present instance few men a thousand years ago could adequately appreciate the nature of the forces tending to the Church's degradation.

Needless to say, the origins of some calamities were obvious, notably the devastation wrought by the Northmen. Yet simply to say, as did the bishops at Reims, that 'some monasteries have been destroyed by heathen' is to convey little sense of the terrors and disruptions involved. In the seventh century, for example, the monks of St Philibert had established themselves at Noirmoutier, an island off the mouth of the Loire in the Bay of Biscay. By 819, however, Scandinavian raids had begun, and the monks found it necessary to construct a retreat at Dées on the mainland to which they could retire during the raiding months of summer. By 836 the attacks on Noirmoutier became so frequent that the monks transferred permanently to Dées.

In fact, this move proved only a temporary expedient. As the Northmen turned increasingly inland, the monastery was forced again and again to move, first to Cunauld, then to Messay in Poitou, and finally, in 872 or 873, to Saint-Pourçain-sur-Sioule. Nevertheless, the devastation of the raiders pursued the wanderers of St Philibert even there, so in 875 they again picked up their relics and trekked all the way across the mountainous vastness of central France to the fortified town of Tournus in Burgundy. Only there did they find the peace and security they had sought for so long.

It goes without saying that the experiences of the monks of St Philibert were far from unique. As repositories of the gifts of the faithful, churches and monasteries naturally became primary targets for attack, and few of those subjected to assault came through the ordeal in any condition to resume positions of spiritual and material prominence. Moreover, even those ecclesiastical establishments fortunate enough to escape barbarian destruction found themselves the object of more insidious designs that proved almost as destructive of religious mission in the long run as had the Scandinavian raids themselves.

Ironically, these designs were largely the consequence, wholly unforeseen, of Carolingian reform. Perhaps hesitating to impose secular jurisdiction on the men and goods of the Church, or perhaps only wishing to avoid some of the expenses of a far-flung bureaucracy, Pepin and Charlemagne had granted rights of immunity to many bishoprics and abbeys, thus freeing them from the supervision of neighbouring counts. Further, not wanting to soil the hands of the clergy with the burdens of earthly care, the Carolingians had insisted that each bishop and abbot appoint a layman to oversee all secular administration. Lastly, acting as much from necessity as from desire for reform, these kings had increasingly granted lands of the Church to their own military supporters; in return, the Church was supposed to be able to impose on all lands in the realm a tithe with which she could support the cost of creating rural parishes for the benefit of an overwhelmingly agricultural populace.

Although these reforms undoubtedly improved the Church in the early ninth century, they rapidly led to her undoing. As the empire disintegrated, lay overseers usurped clerical property while royal retainers soon ceased to recognize the obligations owed to the Church because of their holdings. Tithes too were secularized to the advantage of local aristocrats, and the Church eventually found herself as denuded of power and resources as had the counts whose authority the castellans and viscounts had successfully defied.

Like the rest of society, the Church became fragmented and partially feudalized, but with consequences that were notably more pernicious. In seizing ecclesiastical property, men did not thereby intend the Church's destruction; rather, they were impelled by reasoning not unlike that of those fighting to gain independence of king and count. Self-seeking, but justified by their own conception of law, they struggled to possess that which they considered inherently theirs. Often, however, the acquisition of mere property failed to satisfy them and they did not rest content until they had taken over the very offices of the Church and made them into family holdings.

By the millennium, few bishops and abbots in Europe owed their position to canonical election. Almost without exception prelates could say that they had obtained their offices through nomination or simple appointment by the lord whose family controlled the bishopric or monastery. In some instances a lord would, like Benedict ix, sell vacant offices to the highest bidder, thus guaranteeing himself a handsome income; in others he would use them to endow younger sons, thus providing for their maintenance while at the same time preserving the integrity of family estates. In neither case was much emphasis placed on the spiritual qualifications of the candidates.

Unsurprisingly, this approach to the problem of clerical appointments produced a clergy whose moral and mental attainments were generally low. Church councils complained endlessly of an illiterate and ignorant priesthood, of prelates who gave up the mass for the hunt, and of monks and priests whose days were spent largely in wenching and drunkenness. All discipline seemed to vanish, and it looked for the moment as though lay control were fast driving the Church to her inevitable doom.

Nevertheless, this appearance proved deceiving, primarily because the laity was far from ready to countenance the Church's destruction. Indeed, one could argue in a somewhat paradoxical fashion that religious difficulties arose not from indifference and greed, but more from the misapplication of an intense, though uninformed, religiosity. The typical lord was no atheist; on the contrary, Christ and His saints were most immediate for him, and Marc Bloch was undoubtedly right in asking rhetorically whether anyone could 'fail to recognize in the fear of hell one of the great social forces of the age'.[34] To a surprising extent this fear appears to have provided much of the motivation behind the drive for lay control of appointments. Anxious to gain salvation but understandably nervous about the quality of their own lives, laymen saw in control of the clergy a possible way of improving their standing in the eyes of God. If, for example, a lord could appoint a son, uncle or brother as local bishop or abbot, he could breathe more easily, content in the knowledge that one of his family was in a position of influence, willing and able to grant absolution for sin, thus preparing the way for eternity. Religion became a family affair, and in controlling the Church men saw some hope of controlling God.

In this attitude men displayed more than a little blindness to the imperatives of their faith, but such things serve only to remind us of the extent to which Christianity at the millennium was tinged for most people with a sacramental superstition bordering on the magical. To receive the eucharist and to undergo penance was somehow to purify the soul, regardless of personal attitude; because men understood only externals, they tended increasingly to believe that sacrament and ritual rather than piety provided the safest road to salvation.

Troubling as such an outlook may be, in the end it was to lead to reform. To the primitive mind, the efficacy of magic depends almost entirely on the magician's ability to recite properly his incantations and to perform his rites perfectly; should he slip even in the smallest detail, he risks losing the power

E

to call on those occult forces on which he relies for success. Hence, in so far as the priest in the late ninth to early eleventh centuries was regarded as a kind of magician, he found his religious performance and total life subject to anxious review by a populace fearful lest his sacraments prove invalid. Because contemporary standards of conduct were low, the clergy was allowed more freedom to sin than would be conceivable today, but the limits were there, moral boundaries beyond which no one might venture without risking an angry retribution.

In the event, monasteries became the first objects for reform, and nowhere more than in Burgundy and southern France, areas whose peculiarly advanced forms of political fragmentation had proved unusually devastating to the spiritual life of the Church. As even the pettiest of the local aristocracy contended with each other over the spoils, churches and abbeys found themselves more and more torn apart by the rival claims of those who sought to control them, and under these circumstances the performance of religious duties became well-nigh impossible. Monasteries and cathedrals became the scene of pitched battles; the mass and the hours were but infrequently said; and the conduct of the clergy – especially the monks – plunged to a new low. In a society saturated with a need for sacramental salvation, such conditions were clearly intolerable, and as apprehension and revulsion grew apace, so did the impetus for reform.

Of all the monasteries founded in the course of the tenth century, none is more famous than the Burgundian establishment at Cluny. Chartered in 909 or 910 – the date is disputed – Cluny was to become a model for reform, and by the 1030s and 1040s hundreds, even thousands, of her daughter houses were to be found scattered across the face of Europe. Yet Cluny was far from unique, for this same period saw many independent foundations in Burgundy and Aquitaine, while the monasteries of Germany and Switzerland – places such as Reichenau, Fulda, Hildesheim, and St Michael's – began to flourish under the patronage of the newly re-established emperors. Similarly, in England these were the days of St Dunstan and the revival of Anglo-Saxon monasticism.

Diverse in their origins as these movements for reform may have been, they displayed striking similarities, all of which shed light both on the problems and mentality of the age. Nearly every monastery, for example, owed its foundation or reformation not to the zeal of monks, but rather to the interest and encouragement of some lay patron such as Duke William VI of Aquitaine, who granted Cluny's original charter. From the universality of this phenomenon the extent to which the laity had succeeded in seizing control of the church is apparent.

At the same time, however, the way in which these monasteries were supervised, particularly in southern and eastern France, demonstrates the extent to which all men were also becoming aware of the dangers inherent in lay control. For laymen did not retain authority over the abbeys they founded; nor was it vested in the hands of the local bishops whose appointments the laity similarly controlled. Instead, like Cluny, most reformed monasteries found themselves exempted from all local jurisdiction and placed directly under the rule of the pope.

Although the Rome of John XII and Benedict IX was hardly the town in which to look for leadership in reform, these arrangements made considerable sense at the time. Given the intense rivalries and private wars that were laying waste to the regions where reform was first to appear, new monasteries, if they were to maintain their purity, simply had to be removed from the debilitating effects of local circumstances. And if control had to be lodged elsewhere, what better place than in Rome, the city of saints and martyrs of which poets could still so movingly write? Moreover, despite all the decadence and fragmentation so evident in the Church, men continued to think of it as a unity, mysteriously bound together by the universality of its sacraments, and even if the pope exercised no practical power, he remained the head of Christendom, its Holy Father. Ironic though it may seem, he was the logical custodian of reform.

Lastly, the nature of that reform speaks volumes about the mentality of the times. Cluny and her followers tried not so much to remake the whole man as to shape his external environment so that it would be more in conformity with the standards of Christian conduct. The stated ideal became a return to the *Rule* of St Benedict, to a life of poverty, chastity and obedience lived under the discipline of an abbot to whom was owed unquestioning devotion. As long as regulations were observed and offices said, no monk was likely to be accused of failing his vocation.

Yet few people visiting a Cluniac house would have found it Benedictine in atmosphere. If reform had a true centre, it lay in the reverence accorded the divine liturgy of the mass, and the attention lavished on liturgical details soon separated reformed monasteries from even the best of older establishments. No expense was too great for altar cloth, ciborium and chalice; no vestments were considered too elaborate for the celebrant. Further, the opulence of the setting was matched by a similar opulence in the text of the liturgy itself. Like the loaves and fishes of the Master, prayers and Biblical lessons were multiplied in rich profusion and then adorned with incense, organ and chant until the sacrifice of the mass seemed to fill the whole church with an all-encompassing grandeur that gave concrete expression to the greatness and glory of God.

This, then, was no Puritanical reform, and its excesses were hardly those of asceticism. On the contrary, the reforming impulse arose in the hearts and minds of a people whose magical and superstitious propensities had led them to see in the miracle of the eucharist a transubstantial proof of Heaven's continuing presence and mercy. For mentalities such as these, the sacraments soon became the only meaningful focus of religious expression, and it was reform enough to surround their celebration with a luxury approaching the theatrical while insisting that all monks live up to the letter of their vows. Re-establishment of the proper forms ensured that the sacramental mysteries would continue to have their miraculous powers; after all, they were all that were needed for salvation.

Limited both in aim and in outlook, the reform movement had little impact on the total life of the Church before the second half of the eleventh century. At the millennium Rome was still a sink of crime and corruption; elsewhere in Europe little progress had been made in educating the parish clergy and freeing the bishops from the encumbrances of secular control and worldly interests. On the surface there seemed little change from conditions as they had prevailed a century before.

Nevertheless, beneath the surface momentous changes were brewing. Reform was beginning to create a new spirit in the monasteries and, with it, a trained pool of talent which, although small, was already laying the foundations for the revived civilization of the later Middle Ages. In 972, for example, Gerbert of Reims – the future Sylvester II – established a school where for the first time in centuries logic was studied and attempts were made to recapture the forgotten wisdom of the ancients. Gerbert himself was no more than partially successful in his endeavours, but, imbued with his love of learning, his pupils were later to found most of the educational centres that made possible the renaissance of the twelfth century.

Similarly, by the year 1000 German monasteries under imperial patronage were producing manuscripts, the beauty of whose illuminations has seldom been equalled. Moreover, unlike their Carolingian models, they no longer betrayed a slavish imitation of the classical awkwardly combined with Germanic intrusions; instead, they synthesized elements from both traditions, added a touch of the Byzantine, and in so doing arrived at a style that is totally original and the basis for Romanesque. In this art lies the first sign that medieval men were at last capable of weaving the tangled strands of their cultural inheritance into an integrated and coherent whole.

In short, limited though the reform movement initially appears, it had a significance that far outweighs its original accomplishments. For amidst chaos and deprivation it was the herald and beacon of things to come, a proof that Europe had passed through the worst of its travail and was preparing for growth. Reform may have been superstitious in its origins, a witness to the mentality of the age, but at the same time it contained within it seeds of a new outlook that was eventually to transform the character and quality of European life. By 1000 these seeds had been planted; the next few centuries were to see their development and harvest.

Part 2

The Age of Expansion
1050-1180

4 The Agricultural Revolution

A century ago the Romantic historians (and notably Jules Michelet) developed a rather engaging theory known as the millenary thesis to explain renewed European vitality during the eleventh and twelfth centuries. According to Michelet and his followers, the real cause of earlier hardship and deprivation lay in the generally held belief that the world was going to end in the year 1000; because the millennium and Christ's Second Coming were thought to be nigh, men saw little point in working to alleviate wretched conditions. Instead, resigned to their fate, they went about their daily affairs without lifting a finger to improve a world which was, after all, soon to be irrevocably changed.

As can well be imagined, acceptance of this thesis led many nineteenth-century historians to envisage New Year's Eve, 999 as a night of unspeakable terror. With little regard for the evidence, they conjured up pictures of the whole population of Europe huddled in churches, there fearfully awaiting the dread stroke of midnight while anxiously seeking such scant consolation as religion could offer under the circumstances. Then, of course, midnight came . . . and nothing happened. In this seeming miracle the Romantics were sure that they had discovered the source of European revival. Freed from the burden of everwhelming fear, men found life worth living again; with increasing confidence and hope, they issued forth to build a civilization that was soon to become not unworthy of comparison with classical antiquity itself.

As one might suspect, no one today takes this idea very seriously. Although the Romantics were perfectly correct in pointing out the extent to which general fears were a commonplace in early medieval life, there is really no evidence that any significant number of people thought the world was going to end precisely in 1000; even more to the point, it seems doubtful whether more than a handful had a clear conception of dating or knew with any accuracy even the century in which they lived. For the vast majority of men such things were irrelevant.

Nevertheless, the fact remains that European attitudes experienced a profound transformation after the millennium. In the ninth century, the wintry pessimism of a Sedulius Scotus was not untypical:

> White squalls from the north, amazing to behold,
> Scare us with sudden gusts and threats of cold.
> Earth itself shakes, fearing to be so blown,
> Old ocean mutters, and the hard rocks groan.
> The unruly north wind hollows the vast air,
> Its hoarse voice now whines here, now bellows there.
> Stray milkwhite fleeces thicken into cloud,
> The faded earth puts on a snowy shroud.[35]

By the twelfth century, however, poetry had put on a different mask:

> Spring returns, the long awaited,
>   Laugh, be glad!
> Spring with blossoms decorated,
>   Purple-clad.
> Birds prolong their accords of song there
>   How sweetly!
> Trees renew their youth now,
> Song brings joy in truth now,
>   O completely.[36]

If the millenary thesis no longer suffices to explain this renewal of optimism and hope, other less romantic factors still continue to provide an adequate picture of the change. Of these, none bulks larger than the impact of that agricultural revolution which began strongly to influence the farming techniques of rural Europe from the beginning of the eleventh century. It is not difficult to see why historians have chosen to emphasize it, for only with the appearance of agricultural surpluses did it become possible for men to free themselves not only from subjection to the land but also from those terrors that the constant threat of starvation had created.

Breaking the vicious circle of manorial life proved far from easy. So interconnected were all the problems that one or two improvements could not by themselves overcome the debilitation of the agricultural economy as a whole. To achieve that goal, every aspect of farming had to undergo profound change, and the task was endlessly complicated by a peasant mentality that tended to oppose innovation in any form.

Unsurprisingly, then, this revolution was generations – even centuries – in coming. As far back as Carolingian times its origins can be discerned in the first appearances of the heavy plough. Here was an invention of crucial importance, a device that could, thanks to its share, mouldboard and wheels, break and turn the moist and clayey soils of northern Europe that had defied the best efforts of earlier swing- or scratch-ploughs. Moreover, it pulverized the soil of each furrow so completely that its use ended the need for cross-ploughing, the technique previously employed to gain this end, but only at a cost of twice the effort. Yet, great as the advantages of the heavy plough appear to have been, peasants resisted its adoption for a long time. To some extent their hesitation was the product of innate conservatism, but even more it resulted from the limitations of the implement itself, which needed, for greatest efficiency, to be linked to a number of other innovations. This new plough was terribly expensive, and unless it could be drawn by a team of considerable size, it was apt to prove incredibly slow. Few peasants could afford the expenditure involved, and, even if they could, oxen remained in short supply and methods for harnessing large numbers of them continued unsatisfactory.

Indeed, the heavy plough could achieve its full potential only when coupled with the horse: in horses lay speed, and in speed lay the best hope of increasing agricultural production by allowing the same number of men to bring larger areas of land under cultivation. Here, however, a new set of problems interposed themselves. Unlike oxen, horses required significant amounts of grain to bring them through the winter, and this grain was, needless to say, unavailable. Moreover, their hoofs were tender and subject to injury, while the very nature of their physiques made them even harder than oxen to harness to heavy loads without fear of injury or strangulation.

These difficulties were solved in the course of the ninth and tenth centuries, but initially only on a limited scale. If hoofs were easily damaged, the solution proved to be the horseshoe, seemingly a simple device, but unknown to classical antiquity. Similarly, a great deal of effort went into the development of a horse collar that would transfer the strains of ploughing from the neck to the withers, thus making it possible for a beast safely to exert himself far beyond the limits imposed by previous methods of harnessing.

Once these improvements were effected, it proved relatively easy to create a grain supply adequate to the demands of the winter months. With new techniques and equipment, a peasant could cultivate considerably more land, as well as those richer and more fertile soils whose characteristics had made them unsuitable for exploitation with a swing-plough. Further, because of this very fertility, men discovered that their holdings needed to lie fallow less frequently than had been the custom. As a result, they began to employ a three-field system in which land was put to the plough two years out of three rather than one year out of two. Lastly, new crop rotations were introduced that encouraged the sowing of one field of summer crops – basically the 'oats, pease, beans and barley' of *Mother Goose* – and of another to winter ones, especially wheat and rye. Only the third field was left fallow.

That productivity rose enormously under this system there can be no doubt. More fertile soil meant greater harvests, and the combination of summer and winter crops provided not only a food supply that was more frequently available, but also a work schedule in which the onerous labour of

73

ploughing and harvesting were more evenly spread throughout the year. Because planting now took place in both fall and spring, one plough and team could cultivate twice as much land as under a single planting cycle, and thanks to the greater speed of the horse, this task was more rapidly accomplished.

What these changes meant in practical terms was that, given a manor of constant size, fewer ploughs and draught animals were needed to exploit the land. In other words, even though equipment became increasingly expensive, its greater efficiency probably led to a smaller total capital outlay. Moreover, productive acreage rose from one half to two thirds of the land available, and in this growth there proved to be a number of other, less obvious savings. It was becoming more and more common to plough fallow fields twice a year, once in spring and again in midsummer; consequently, as the proportion of fallow was reduced, the amount of ploughing required was reduced even further. Similarly, the elimination of any necessity for cross-ploughing also led to the same result: greater harvests for less work. In turn, more grain meant that more animals, especially horses, could be brought through the winter. Draught animals ceased to be in short supply, and their growing numbers provided not only a possible source of animal protein for the human diet, but also abundant quantities of manure with which to replenish the soil.

In the eleventh century the full implications of this slow revolution began at last to be clear. Only then were its various aspects finally moulded into a coherent system whose benefits were sufficiently obvious to overcome the resistance to change of even the most conservative of peasants. At no time, however, were the new methods universally adopted, for they were clearly unsuited to regions with poor soil and harsh climates. Nevertheless, by mid-century they were in common enough use that it is fair to say that Europe had broken free from the vicious circle of deprivation and want to which she had previously been held in thrall. At long last she and her inhabitants had gained the possibility of a fuller life.

On the manor, this possibility frequently took the form of a technological inventiveness aimed at further reducing the dependence on human muscle power. Large mills were built, with grinding stones powered by oxen and water wheels; gear trains, windlasses and pulleys were developed that allowed men and beasts alike to multiply the effectiveness of their strength; even the wind was harnessed and put to work as a pumper of water and grinder of grain. We in the twentieth century tend unconsciously to assume that machines and other labour-saving devices are entirely the product of modern ingenuity, but the inventions of the Middle Ages prove that we are wrong. Our mistake is blindly to regard the machinery of an eleventh-century water mill as technologically unremarkable, whereas it seemed far otherwise to women whose days had hitherto been filled with the arduous drudgery of grinding meal and flour by hand; for them, it was both remarkable and a great blessing. In short, awe-inspiring as the so-called miracle of automation may be, it is little more than the most recent expression of man's eternal quest for ways to rid himself of endless, repetitive toil.

Be that as it may, technology and the agricultural revolution were soon to transform the face of Europe. With food supplies again plentiful, fewer people starved or became subject to wasting dietary diseases. As a result, the population began to rise. At the millennium, for example, France was unable to support more than six to eight million inhabitants; by the early fourteenth century, on the other hand, this figure had swollen to some eighteen million or more. The French experience was not untypical; everywhere men were increasing in vitality and numbers.

As population grew, it quickly exceeded the productive capacities of the land previously under cultivation. No longer could peasants look forward to taking over and maintaining their fathers' holdings; now there were simply too many heirs for these plots to support, so for the first time in centuries men were forced to open new land and greatly to increase the amount of acreage actually put to the plough. Because most manors contained a surplus of pasture, woodlands and waste that was easily converted to agricultural production, expansion could initially take place without much change in attitude and outlook. Even in clearing new land, men remained close to those places that had given them birth, thereby ensuring a continuity in circumstances that prevented most peasants from questioning the customs and assumptions that had always governed their lives.

With the passage of time, however, manorial surpluses disappeared and men were forced to look farther and farther afield for new holdings. Like the pioneer farmers of nineteenth-century America, the peasantry of the eleventh and twelfth centuries showed an increasing willingness to abandon ancestral homes and to seek its fortune in the wilderness. Trackless wastes that had never known the gentling hand of man became the goal of settlers determined to wrest a living from even the most unpromising of soils. Once realized, the opportunities seemed endless: much of England and France remained to be colonized, and beyond the Rhine and the Elbe there stretched the vast expanses of Germany and Slavdom, empty spaces that appeared almost to cry out in their need for development.

Probably never before or since has Europe experienced migration on a scale approaching that of the two centuries following the millennium. This was the period of the Germanic *Drang nach Osten* and the Christian reconquest of Spain, of Viking settlements in North America and crusading kingdoms in the East. People were on the move, and Europe with them. All this bustling activity involved much that was anarchic and chaotic, but at the same time there were often striking indications of shrewd planning. In Holland, for example, Cistercian monks took the lead in developing methods for reclaiming land from the sea. First, lay brethren built dikes, after which windmills were set to work, pumping out the unwanted water. Even when dry, however, the fields remained salty and unfit for planting, so next they were turned into sheep pasture for periods as long as seven years. At that point, oxen replaced the sheep, and the fields were left for their grazing until the cumulative effect of the constant manuring at last made the soil fit for cultivation. Only then was the land put to the plough.

Because projects like the reclamation of Holland required immense amounts of planning and capital, they probably were more the exception than the rule. Only the wealthiest of lords or monastic houses could afford to undertake them. Much more common were instances in which a lord, having extra land that he wished to develop, simply issued charters inviting all those who were interested to come and take part in the effort. In these documents all the advertising skills of the rental agent first made their appearance: site, climate and soil conditions were seductively described; some lords even went so far as to include rough diagrams of the neat villages that they intended to build. Little wonder that these appeals proved most attractive to peasants who very recently had endured quite different circumstances.

In some cases, of course, no invitations were necessary: settlers simply tried to take over tracts of land unpeopled by others. Such appears to be the explanation for a charter issued by the bishop of Hamburg in 1106:

1. In the name of the holy and undivided Trinity. Frederick, by the grace of God bishop of Hamburg, to all the faithful in Christ, gives a perpetual benediction. We wish to make known to all the agreement which certain people living this side of the Rhine, who are called Hollanders, have made with us.
2. These men came to us and earnestly begged us to grant them certain lands in our bishopric, which are uncultivated, swampy, and useless to our people. We have consulted our subjects about this and, considering that this would be profitable to us and to our successors, have granted their request.
3. The agreement was made that they should pay us every one *denarius* [i.e. one penny] for every hide of land. . . . We also grant them the streams which flow through this land.
4. They agreed to give the tithe according to our decree, that is, every eleventh sheaf of grain, every tenth lamb, every tenth pig, every tenth goat, every tenth goose, and a tenth of the honey and of the flax. For every colt they shall pay a *denarius* on St Martin's day, and for every calf an obol [i.e. a halfpenny]. . . .[37]

When compared to conditions prevailing only a century earlier, the striking feature of this document is the sharp diminution in the amount of rent and services demanded of those seeking to use the land. The bishop requires neither labour nor *corvées* on his own holdings, and he limits his financial rewards to a modest rent plus payment of the accustomed tithe. Doubtless these terms resulted partly from the belief that the land in question was 'uncultivated, swampy, and useless' to all save Hollanders, but at the same time their generosity reflects pressures and tendencies that were far from being restricted to the poorer districts of the diocese of Hamburg.

For all over Europe the expansion of agriculture had led inevitably to fierce competition for labour. Although a rising population meant that new production was absolutely essential, the fact of the matter was that a particular tract of land was much more apt to be cleared and developed if the peasantry was given suitable rewards. Consequently, since a lord could not reasonably expect to lure men from their old homes unless he could provide good motives for moving, he was forced to reduce his demands and offer terms significantly more attractive than those generally prevailing. Thus a lord might agree to forego all rents during the first few years of tenancy; further, he might eliminate all labour services while stipulating that he himself would provide without charge such necessities as seed corn, breeding stock, and expensive equipment. Lastly, he might limit payments in kind to a percentage of the crop actually harvested, thereby assuring his tenants that their efforts would not go totally unrewarded even in times of adverse conditions.

Whatever the inducements offered – and they were many and varied – peasants responded with alacrity. The opportunity to escape servile conditions proved greater than most tenants could resist. Indeed, many found that the new lands were not alone in their promise of a fresh start under favourable circumstances. During the course of the eleventh century the long dormant cities of Europe began at last to show signs of revival, and as they grew, their commerce and industry were also forced to compete for their share of a labour supply which, thanks to the nature of things, could come only from the rural and agricultural countryside.

These developments placed the lords of established manors in a difficult position. In theory, most of their peasants were serfs, legally unfree and tied to the soil: men over whom they had had the power of life and death and from whom they had been accustomed to extract the last margin of profit. In practice, however, lords soon found it impossible in these new times to retain tenants who had become convinced that greater opportunities lay elsewhere; serfs tended simply to slip away, seldom to be tracked down and recaptured. Unable to enforce their theoretical rights successfully, lords had in the end to meet the competition by reducing the burdens of tenure. As in the case of new lands, rents were lowered; labour services and *corvées* were abolished or commuted; and the peasantry was promised a wide variety of other inducements designed to keep it content on the lands it had traditionally tilled. In short, the agricultural revolution brought in its train a general amelioration of peasant conditions, and not just improvements for those hardy enough to tempt fate by venturing forth into the wilderness.

Moreover, manorial life was further transformed by two other factors: the reappearance of a money economy and the growth of agricultural specialization, changes closely linked to the rise of the towns and whose impact helped to create the final features of a rural society that was to endure on the continent with surprisingly few modifications right down to the time of the French Revolution. First and foremost, by the start of the twelfth century money had again become common. Although initially an urban and commercial phenomenon, its use spread gradually to the countryside where its introduction served to cap all the liberalizing tendencies of the agricultural revolution. Given the diminished rents that the competition for labour had entailed, and given the increasing luxuries to which the upper classes aspired, manorial lords understandably found themselves more and more pressed in trying to maintain incomes sufficient for their needs. Unsurprisingly, then, the nobility (and by the twelfth century the aristocracy had at last become one) proved not unwilling to grant further favours to the peasantry in return for hard cash. Payments in kind were converted into monetary rents; services could be bought off in coin; and – possibly most important of all, at least psychologically – serfs were allowed to buy their freedom, assuming they could save up the required fee.

For the peasants, this economic change had a number of far-reaching implications. Since the twelfth and thirteenth centuries were a period of mounting inflation, those tenants fortunate or shrewd enough to have commuted their obligations into fixed monetary rents discovered that a smaller and smaller percentage of the income received for their crops had to be paid to their lords. In turn, this made it easier to save up the sums needed to purchase emancipation. As a result, probably no more than ten per cent of the French farming population were serfs by the middle of the thirteenth century, whereas fully ninety per cent had lived under servile conditions three hundred years earlier. It was at this time, one suspects, that the peasantry first developed the propensity for hoarding its coins against that unknown day of disaster on which ready cash might enable it to buy its salvation.

The very fact that agriculture revolved increasingly around the exchange of money led inevitably to specialized production. In previous centuries all manors had been more or less self-sufficient, growing and making nearly everything needed for human existence; in the absence of commerce and trade, there was no other choice. Once agriculture became part of a money economy, however, peasants were naturally encouraged to raise only those crops that promised the highest return. Thus in Flanders the growth of great textile towns created immense demands for wool, flax and dyestuffs such as woad, products in which the surrounding countryside began quickly to specialize. In the newly colonized territories east of the Elbe, access to the Baltic made profitable the raising and shipping of wheat to those areas where rapid urbanization had given rise to expanding markets. Similarly, soil, climate and geography caused much of southern France to turn to cultivation of the vine, while England too was not without her speciality: it was during the twelfth century that one could first discern the emergence of the wool trade, on which her future wealth would so largely be founded.

Though men scarcely realized it at the time, they were deeply engaged in the creation of an interdependent, European-wide economy that was forever to replace the self-sufficiency of the manor. The rural population no longer had to rely exclusively on the fruits of its own labours; if goods were desired that it neither made nor raised, growing numbers of peddlars, fairs and market towns were appearing which could easily supply its needs from sources of production scattered all over the continent – and even beyond. Peasants' horizons that had once stopped at the borders of their fields now stretched out, at least in a vague way, until they encompassed the whole of Europe.

Nevertheless, great as were the changes brought by the agricultural revolution, it would be wrong to suppose that the life of the average peasant had been totally transformed. Constant and unending toil was still required for survival, and in outlook most of the inhabitants of the countryside remained incredibly superstitious. Many girls believed that they could discover the names of their future husbands by stretching a newly spun thread across the entrances to their homes: he who broke the thread would invariably prove to have the same first name as the man eventually married. In the same way, others were certain that flax left on the distaff over a Sunday would make unbleachable linen, or that cows would kick over the milk-pails unless greeted with the salutation: 'God and St Bridget bless you'. Wakes were a time for the telling of legends and ghost stories, while most villages could lay claim to a witch. Continuity with the heritage of the past was not easily severed.

Yet conditions had unquestionably improved. In personal terms, the majority of the peasantry now had its freedom, and few were subjected to the harsh seigneurial demands that had characterized the world in 1000. If a thirteenth-century poem, *De l'Oustillement au Vilain*, can be believed, creature comforts were also more numerous, notably in the home, which was larger, better made, and occasionally equipped with both chimney and oven. Animals were now confined to a shed at the rear, and separate buildings were provided for the storing of grain, hay and straw. The family bedstead (there was still only one) occupied a place close to the hearth, while everywhere tools and cooking utensils alike gave proof that the Iron Age had finally come to the peasants of Europe. Moreover, even though hard labour continued to fill the greater part of each day, rising productivity had made possible the creation of more leisure time when cares could be safely abandoned for the pleasures of the moment. As a city-dweller of a somewhat later period described such an occasion, it takes on a timeless simplicity that transcends the centuries:

Once, having had to retire into the country more conveniently and uninterruptedly to finish some business, as I was walking on a particular holiday I came to a neighbouring village where the greater part of the old and young men were assembled in groups of separate ages. . . . The young were practising the bow, jumping, wrestling, running races, and playing other games. The old were looking on, some sitting under an oak, with their legs crossed, and their hats lowered over their eyes, others leaning on their elbows criticizing every performance, and refreshing the memory of their own youth, and taking a lively interest in seeing the gambols of the young.[38]

Similar holiday scenes are still to be found in the villages of Europe today.

Be that as it may, the evidence appears conclusive that while the peasants of the eleventh and twelfth centuries led a life far removed from luxury and ease, at least their existence was no longer filled with the kinds of terror and foreboding that had so poisoned the atmosphere in earlier times. The threat of starvation had receded, and with its passing men found themselves better able to leave the lands of their birth. Mobility and travel increased; geographical knowledge improved; and the world, which had once seemed an evil and dangerous place, now took on the guise of a new Garden of Eden. Witches and hobgoblins might continue to flourish in peasant mythology, but in the stories that arose in this period they were gradually supplanted by different interests and themes, ones that for the first time emphasized an enjoyment of nature and a shrewd amusement with the foibles of man.

Perhaps no tale better illustrates the point than *Reynard the Fox*, a fable that quickly achieved unrivalled popularity. Reynard, of course, epitomizes all those who succeed by using their wits, and in most versions of the story he easily outsmarts the other animals with a show of sweet reasonableness and cunning that rapidly dispels their gravest suspicions. In most incidents Reynard is no more than the fun-filled trickster, the rogue who can persuade the wife of Isegrim the wolf to fish with her tail in a river that is rapidly turning to ice or who can entice Bruin the bear to eat so much of the priest's food that the poor beast becomes much too fat for escape. On other occasions, however, his wits must be put to more serious ends: When Noble the lion, king of the beasts, is about to hang him for thievery and treason, Reynard escapes the noose only by conjuring up for the royal avarice a vision of treasure whose hiding place he alone knows; while losing in mortal combat to a furious Isegrim, he suddenly offers to become a pilgrim and to pray for Isegrim's soul – and then seizes the initiative when the unfortunate wolf, moved by religious sentiment, momentarily relaxes his grip. For Reynard, no strategem is too outrageous, and in the end his cunning conquers all: convinced that the wily fox has no equal, Noble appoints him royal judge, a post in which he happily spends the rest of his days. As for a moral, most narrators were quick to supply one:

Think well, all ye who have heard this story, for no good man has been blamed in it. Thus, if any of you have erred as Reynard did, look well to your lives and amend them.

Clearly enough, a tale like *Reynard the Fox* introduced a new element into what had hitherto been the generally gloomy canon of medieval popular literature. Filled with barbed social commentary and a bubbling zest for life, *Reynard* was a fable that spoke to the optimist in man, telling him that with brains, skill and ambition he could yet be the master of his fate. No more was the lord to be feared; instead, he was lampooned and outwitted. Indeed, so lacking in danger had the whole physical universe become that it could now comfortably treat even the most ferocious of beasts as vehicles for the depiction of human folly, a technique that had scarcely been used since the times of classical antiquity. In short, *Reynard the Fox* is the imaginative creation of a populace freed at last from the thralldom of nature and fully at home in its world.

Who, then, shall say that Michelet and the Romantics were entirely mistaken? Though wrong in their facts, their genius was first to perceive the change in spirit that came across Europe after the year 1000. Theirs was no mean achievement, for it was, after all, the Romantic interpretation that helped to produce a more serious examination of the forces lying behind continental revival. And if the harrowing vision of New Year's Eve, 999 has now been replaced by endless discussions of horse collars, windmills and ploughs, there is little reason to suppose that the future will find these explanations any less quaint than the millenary thesis that preceded them. Such are the ways of History.

5 The Rise of the Towns

Not least among the consequences of the agricultural revolution was the rise of the towns, for with the creation of an adequate food supply men could again contemplate the possibility of careers more independent of the land and its products. Although urban centres were initially small, they expanded rapidly until, by the end of the twelfth century, they dotted the landscape with a profusion far exceeding anything known at the height of the Roman Empire. During the eleventh century, however, much of Europe remained profoundly rural, tied to the soil, and ignorant of the advantages of city living. For a countryman, the first visit to a teeming metropolis is always an overwhelming experience, and nowhere, perhaps, is the exhilaration of such an encounter better captured than in Fulcher of Chartres' account of his arrival at Constantinople as a member of the First Crusade in 1097:

Oh, what a great and beautiful city is Constantinople! How many churches and palaces it contains, fashioned with wonderful skill! How many wonderful things may be seen even in the streets or courts! It would be too tedious to enumerate what wealth there is there of every kind, of gold, of silver, of every kind of robes, and of holy relics. There traders at all times bring by boat all the necessities of man. They have, I judge, about twenty thousand eunuchs constantly living there.[39]

Even as late as the opening of the thirteenth century, Constantinople retained its capacity to awe, and Robert of Clari could report that those on the Fourth Crusade 'regarded the great size of the city, which was so long and so wide, and marvelled at it exceedingly'.[40] For Robert, the treasures of Constantinople surpassed those of Alexander and Charlemagne, and nothing approaching its wealth could be found even 'in the forty richest cities of the world.'[41] Like Fulcher of Chartres, he found that any attempt to describe its wonders quickly exhausted the limited range of his vocabulary:

All these marvels which I have recounted to you here and still a great many more than we could recount, the French found in Constantinople after they had captured it, nor do I think, for my part, that any man on earth could number all the abbeys of the city, so many there were, both of monks and of nuns, aside from the other churches outside the city. And it was reckoned that there were in the city a good thirty thousand priests, both monks and others. Now about the rest of the Greeks, high and low, rich and poor, about the size of the city, about the palaces and the other marvels that are there, we shall leave off telling you. For no man on earth, however long he might have lived in the city, could number them or recount them to you. And if anyone should recount to you the hundredth part of the richness and the beauty and the nobility that was found in the abbeys and in the churches and in the palaces and in the city, it would seem like a lie and you would not believe it.[42]

Others, however, were quick to sense the seamier side of the Byzantine capital, and in their accounts revulsion with urban conditions was allowed to outweigh even the acknowledged beauties of the city. In this regard, the reactions of Odo of Deuil in the 1140s were entirely typical:

The city itself is squalid and fetid and in many places harmed by permanent darkness, for the wealthy overshadow the streets with buildings and leave these dirty, dark places to the poor and to travellers; there murders and robberies and other crimes which love the darkness are committed. Moreover, since people live lawlessly in this city, which has as many lords as rich men and almost as many thieves as poor men, a criminal knows neither fear nor shame, because crime is not punished by law and never entirely comes to light. In every respect she exceeds moderation: for, just as she surpasses other cities in wealth, so, too, does she surpass them in vice.[43]

Varied as were these impressions of the richest town in Christendom, they may nevertheless be taken as an accurate reflection of the kinds of response that all urban centres were apt to call forth from their visitors. For some, cities were a place of challenge and excitement, bustling hives of activity where both pleasure and wealth could be sought. For others, they seemed little more than pigsties, dank cesspools whose stench and overcrowded conditions were enough to prevent any sensible man from living in them. And these reactions were not the product of size alone, for during the twelfth century they became a commonplace throughout the West, none of whose towns could even begin to approach Constantinople in the extent of its population. In all the Middle Ages, for example, London never contained more than forty thousand inhabitants, and yet William Fitz-Stephen could write about its advantages in 1173 with an enthusiasm scarcely exceeded by the admirers of Byzantium itself:

Among the noble cities of the world that Fame celebrates the City of London of the Kingdom of the English is the one seat that pours out its fame more widely, sends to farther lands its wealth and trade, lifts its head higher than the rest. It is happy in the healthiness of its air, in the Christian religion, in the strength of its defences, the nature of its site, the honour of its citizens, the modesty of its matrons; pleasant in sports; fruitful of noble men. . . .

Those engaged in the several kinds of business, sellers of several things, contractors for several kinds of work, are distributed every morning into their several localities and shops. Besides, there is in London on the river bank, among the wines in ships and cellars sold by the vintners, a public cook shop; there eatables are to be found every day, according to the season, dishes of meat, roast, fried and boiled, great and small fish, coarser meats for the poor, more delicate for the rich, of game, fowls, and small birds. . . . Outside one of the gates there, immediately in the suburb, is a certain field, smooth [i.e., Smith] field in fact and name. Every Friday, unless it be a higher day of appointed solemnity, there is in it a famous show of noble horses for sale. . . . In another part of the field stand by themselves the goods proper to rustics, implements of husbandry, swine with long flanks, cows with full udders, oxen of bulk immense, and woolly flocks. . . . To this city from every nation under heaven merchants delight to bring their trade by sea. . . . I do not think there is a city with more commendable customs of church attendance, honour to God's ordinances, keeping sacred festivals, almsgiving, hospitality, confirming betrothals, contracting marriages, celebration of nuptials, preparing feasts, cheering the guests, and also in care for funerals and the interment of the dead. The only pests of London are the immoderate drinking of fools and the frequency of fires.[44]

Whatever the validity of William's description – and there is much to be said in its favour – his very exuberance suggests the kind of widening gulf that was beginning to separate urban from country living. Newly created though the bourgeoisie may have been, the singularity of its circumstances led quickly to the development of manners and morals greatly at variance with those of peasantry and nobility alike. For the city imposed a different set of assumptions from those traditional on the manor. To cite only the most obvious example, towns were man-made whereas the countryside was not; as a result, their environment tended to encourage the belief that prosperity in business affairs depended almost exclusively on such personal qualities as intelligence, energy and resourcefulness. Unlike the peasant, whose harvest was constantly threatened by climatic catastrophes, the bourgeois could seldom appeal to droughts, blights and other natural disasters as an explanation of his shortcomings: if he failed, he could find the cause only in his own stupidity – just as his successes were to be attributed to his abilities.

In short, towns seemed much more man-centred than the countryside. The very rapidity of their rise stood as a monument to human creativity, and it should be hardly surprising to discover the extent to which a raw, boisterous enthusiasm pervaded their outlook. Man had yet to become the measure of all things, but for the city-dweller the fear of divine intervention had clearly receded, and he saw little danger in enjoying the worldly pleasures of this life without worrying overmuch about the spiritual consequences. As the Archpoet of Cologne confessed, probably in the 1160s:

Down the primrose path I post
  Straight to Satan's grotto,
Shunning virtue, doing most
  Things that I ought not to:
Little Hope of heaven I boast,
  Charmed by pleasure's otto:
Since the soul is bound to roast
  Save the skin's my motto. . . .

Much too hard it is, I find,
  So to change my essence
As to keep a virgin mind
  In a virgin's presence.
Rigid laws can never bind
  Youth to acquiescence;
Light o' loves must seek their kind,
  Bodies take their pleasance.

Who that in a bonfire falls
  Is not scorched by flame there?
Who can leave Pavia's walls
  Pure as when he came there?
Venus' beckoning finger calls
  Youths with sportive aims there,
Eyes make captive willing thralls,
  Faces hunt for game there. . . .

Next, I'm called in terms precise
  Monstrous fond of gaming;
Losing all my clothes at dice
  Gains me this worth naming:
While outside I'm cool as ice,
  Inwardly I'm flaming,
Then with daintiest device
  Poems and songs I'm framing. . . .

My intention is to die
  In the tavern drinking;
Wine must be at hand, for I
  Want it when I'm sinking.
Angels when they come shall cry,
  At my frailties winking:
'Spare this drunkard, God, he's high,
  Absolutely stinking!'[45]

In the twelfth century, then, there was about the towns and cities of Europe an atmosphere of confident, devil-may-care exuberance. Life was to be enjoyed, and if that involved sins of the flesh, there was remarkable optimism about the eventual outcome. Yet such had not always been the case, and to understand fully the nature of the urban outlook in all its complexities, one must return to the beginning and examine the travails of a still nascent bourgeoisie as it struggled to establish a place for itself in a society that was initially far from friendly.

First of all, it would be wrong to assume that commerce and trade had totally disappeared in the West after the fall of Rome. Cities may well have died except as centres of episcopal and governmental administration, but there seems always to have been a limited number of pedlars, usually Jewish or Syrian in origin, who continued to wander the byways of Europe, hawking their wares and bringing news of an outside world to people for whom it must have had little more than a mythic, enchanted existence. Insignificant as these itinerant merchants may initially appear, they were the cadres for future generations. Moreover, cities had survived in the East, and to those who knew of them, places such as Constantinople, Baghdad and Damascus provided continuing lessons on the acquisition of wealth. Finally, possibly proving that the line separating piracy from commerce has never been clear, even the depredations of the Vikings had their salutary effects, for the disposal of booty led to the development of a rudimentary system of Northern trade that later merchants proved eager to exploit.

Though small and inadequate, these were the foundations on which urban expansion was built. Towns began to show signs of life after the middle of the tenth century, and for understandable reasons: the second wave of barbarian invasions had ended; a modicum of peace had been restored; and the agricultural revolution was slowly making it possible to acquire the necessary food supplies. In Italy, Venice was the first to stir, stimulated, no doubt, by her proximity to Byzantium, but other towns soon followed. The first half of the eleventh century saw Pisa, Genoa and Venice not only thriving, but actually seizing control of the Mediterranean from the Muslims who had successfully dominated it for over three hundred years. At almost the same time, a similar vitality appeared in northern Europe. Flemish woollens, though peasant-made, had long enjoyed a high reputation: so much so, in fact, that when the legendary Harun-al-Rashid sent Charlemagne an elephant, the Frankish monarch could think of nothing better to give in return than several bolts of this precious cloth. In other words, Flanders had a product of value, and by 1050 its manufacture was being increasingly concentrated in urban centres whose very names – Ghent, Bruges, Lille, Douai, Antwerp – were soon to become synonymous with prosperity and wealth.

For all their future greatness, few towns had an easy birth. If commercial affairs were in any way to succeed, merchants needed a number of guarantees, above all freedom to travel and security from devastating attack. Because towns depended on the exchange of goods, they tended necessarily to grow up along routes of natural communication, first on the shores of the sea and then inland, along the banks of the great rivers. Some, like Milan and Lyon, were little more than Roman foundations revived, while others were original creations; all other things being equal, however, towns seemed more apt to flourish in places where a castle or some form of natural protection could provide for their defence. No matter where towns were established, they faced a multitude of difficulties. No land was freely available just for the asking; there was always a lord, and not infrequently his attitude toward commerce proved less than receptive. From his point of view, especially if he were a cleric, the advent of the bourgeoisie was at best a mixed blessing. Trade might bring revenues and luxury goods such as he could scarcely imagine, but at the same time he quickly discovered that city-dwellers were likely to be endless in their demands. They sought lordly protection, wherever they might be; they insisted on independent town governments and personal liberty; they tried to deny the jurisdiction of seigneurial courts, whose feudal and manorial laws were hardly applicable to commercial transactions. And to bishops and abbots, not least among the bourgeois faults was a love of gain and acceptance of usury.

Faced by implicit hostility the inhabitants of each town began to create sworn associations. In some instances, leading merchants formed a gild, all of whose members were bound to aid each other in need and to protect the whole community from the incursions of strangers. In other cases, the entire population was involved, with every male over fifteen being sworn to keep the peace and to join the communal militia when wrongdoers threatened. Yet, whatever the specific forms that were actually chosen, the groups thus created soon found themselves the effective government of the towns.

In time, many lords, confronted by a *fait accompli*, simply decided to make the best of a bad situation and issued charters in which town liberties were recognized, but always in return for annual payments that would compensate for seigneurial losses while increasing the sense of lordly prestige. In France and on much of the continent, any powerful lord could issue such charters, but in England they remained a royal prerogative. Thus it was Henry I himself in the early twelfth century who acknowledged that Newcastle-upon-Tyne had the following rights:

The burgesses may distrain foreigners within their market and without, and within their homes and without, and within their borough and without, and they may do this without the permission of the [royal] reeve. . . .

If a burgess shall lend anything in the borough to someone dwelling outside, the debtor shall pay back the debt if he admits it, or otherwise do right in the court of the borough.

Pleas which arise in the borough shall there be held and concluded except those which belong to the king's crown.

If a burgess shall be sued in respect of any plaint he shall not plead outside the borough except for defect of court; nor need he answer, except at a stated time and place. . . .

If a ship comes to the Tyne and wishes to unload, it shall be permitted to the burgesses to purchase what they please. . . .

If a burgess have a son in his house and at his table, his son shall have the same liberty as his father.

If a villein come to reside in the borough, and shall remain as a burgess in the borough for a year and a day, he shall thereafter always remain there. . . .

If a burgess sues anyone concerning anything, he cannot force the burgess to trial by battle. . . .

No merchant except a burgess can buy wool or hides or other merchandise outside the town, nor shall he buy them within the town except from burgesses.[46]

These articles are typical of the privileges then being granted all over Europe; with growing frequency the bourgeois found that they were allowed to maintain courts, collect debts, pursue trade and enjoy personal liberty even when it could be proved that their origins were servile. '*Stadtluft macht frei*' went the German legal expression, and it was generally true that town residence of a year and a day relieved the serf of all manorial obligations. Nevertheless, as some of Newcastle's customs make clear, few towns were completely free and open. Only citizens – the burgesses themselves – were permitted to buy in the markets beyond the city walls, and non-citizens attempting to trade within the town were required to purchase their goods from a burgess. Similarly, serfs who came to a town seeking freedom might find the burgesses refusing to take them: when labour was scarce, such men were accepted, but in hard times they were returned to their lords. In short, each town tended solely to foster its own interests. Far from being an age of unfettered free enterprise, the twelfth century was a time of narrow monopoly and urban mercantilism.

Illustrating the point is the growth of the great craft gilds, organizations designed to protect their members by excluding competition and standardizing production procedures. Every trade had its gild, among them the weavers of London, men to whom Henry II found it profitable to issue a charter in the early years of his reign:

Henry, by the grace of God, king of England, duke of Normany and Aquitaine, count of Anjou, to the bishops, justiciars, sheriffs, barons, and all his servants and liegemen of London, greeting. Know that I have granted to the weavers of London to have their gild in London with all the liberties and customs which they had in the time of King Henry, my grandfather. Let no one carry on this occupation unless by their permission, and unless he belong to their gild, within the city, or in Southwark, or in the other places pertaining to London, other than those who were wont to do so in the time of King Henry, my grandfather. Wherefore I will and firmly order that they shall everywhere legally carry on their business, and that they shall have all the aforementioned things as well and peacefully and freely and honourably and entirely as ever they had them in the time of King Henry, my

The Varieties of Medieval Experience

A burial at Tournai (1349). The vision of death was always present in the Middle Ages, but never more strikingly than at the time of the Black Death.

Even the clothes of the afflicted were burnt, but to little avail.

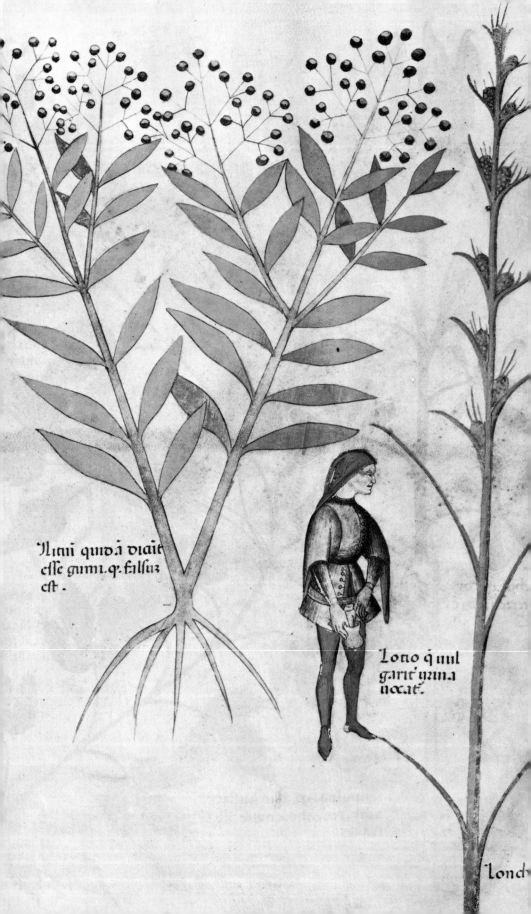

Ilimi quida diait
esse gumi. q̃. falsuz
est .

Iomo q̃ uul
garit' urina
uocat.

londi

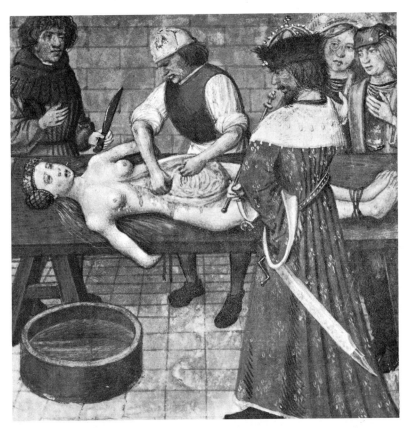

Men sought medicinal herbs for relief and freely produced specimens for examination (*left*), but doctors were crude in their methods (*top*), and even the slightly injured ran risks in visiting them (*immediately above*).

Some men diverted themselves in sport, hunting both birds and beasts (*above and top right*), but others, like King John, sought human quarry (*bottom right*, Matthew Paris manuscript, 1216).

. aɒ uſas uɪnɒıs .

. aɒ uſaıs qɒ alıo noıͣ mıſch .
. ct arnech apellat .

Men had recourse to the solace of religion (*left*), or to direct action, as in the Peasants' Revolt, led by Wat Tyler and John Ball (*below*).

For some, like Chaucer's Wife of Bath, the burdens of life hardly diminished its joys and pleasures (*top*), and his Pardoner profited from the folly of others (*immediately above*).

A tenth-century comb and a fourteenth-century jug testify to the everyday activities that bound people of all experiences together.

grandfather; provided always that for this privilege they pay me each year 2 marks of gold at Michaelmas. And I forbid anyone to do them injury or insult in respect of this on pain of 10 pounds forfeiture. Witness: Thomas [Becket] of Canterbury: Warin fitz Gerold. At Winchester.[47]

Not every town, however, proved as fortunate in its lords as did London and Newcastle-upon-Tyne. On occasion, nobles and ecclesiastics attempted to dominate their citizens and deny them their rights, and when they did, there was apt to be trouble. In 1074, for example, the archbishop of Cologne was entertaining the bishop of Münster, and at the time of the latter's departure, the archbishop ordered his servants to find a boat for the trip. But Lambert of Hersfeld should continue the tale:

They looked all about, and finally found a good boat which belonged to a rich merchant of the city, and demanded it for the archbishop's use. . . . The merchant's servants hastily ran to their lord and told him what had happened to the boat, and asked him what they should do. The merchant had a son who was both bold and strong. He was related to the great families of the city, and, because of his character, very popular. He hastily collected his servants, and as many of the young men of the city as he could, rushed to the boat, ordered the servants of the archbishop to get out of it, and violently ejected them from it. The advocate of the city was called in, but his arrival only increased the tumult, and the merchant's son drove him off and put him to flight. The friends of both parties seized their arms and came to their aid, and it looked as if there was going to be a great battle fought in the city.[48]

In this instance, the archbishop was finally able to restore order, but others were less fortunate. In 1070 the people of Le Mans formed a commune and rose against their lord; as the hostile episcopal chronicler reported ensuing events:

Made bold by this conspiracy they began to commit innumerable crimes, condemning many people indiscriminately and without cause, blinding some for the smallest reasons and, horrible to say, hanging others for insignificant faults. They even burned the strongholds of the area during Lent, and what is worse during the period of the Passion of Our Lord. And all this they did without reason.[49]

Similarly, when the bishop of Laon attempted in 1112 to suppress its commune and even had the temerity to levy a tax of seven hundred pounds to cover his expenses for gaining permission from Henry I for his actions, the town erupted in the midst of a religious procession, and to the shouts of 'Commune! Commune!' everyone went running to find the bishop. Discovered cowering in a wine butt, the poor man was dragged forth and summarily hacked to pieces. Complete order did not return until 1116 or 1117, and then only because the bourgeois had become finally convinced that the rights of their commune would be fully respected. Obviously, municipal liberties were not lightly to be tampered with, and he who attempted to change them did so at his own peril.

Thus, if there was an atmosphere of confident, carefree exuberance about the cities of twelfth-century Europe, it reflected much more than the spontaneous, innocent outpourings of a class newly endowed with wealth. Rather, the tumultuous vitality of the towns owed not a little to the very difficulties of their struggle for recognition and power. The enthusiasms of the bourgeoisie were those of a class untamed, of men who worked hard and played hard in a world whose harsh, competitive challenges they had found they could master. Quick to anger, but equally quick to show either penitence or joy, the bourgeois displayed a childish simplicity of character that did not, however, totally mask the raw ferocity of their will to succeed. That they gloried in their abilities, there can be no doubt. The twelfth was the first great century of urban construction, and the splendours of the Romanesque churches that were then fast arising attested not only to the grandeur of God, but also to the skills and prosperity of their makers. This union suggests something of the undifferentiated approach of the age, one that could see little distinction among the various spheres of its activities. Although Abelard may have begun as a teacher in Paris, interested in the nature of God, he apparently saw no conflict between theology and his relations with Heloïse; moreover, his very decision to name their child Astrolabus in honour of the newly developed navigational aid stands as a curious proof of the extent to which even the greatest speculative mind of the day could exult in practical, human invention.

Yet, in spite of all those features of life that forever separate the twelfth century from the twentieth, there nevertheless began to emerge in the towns certain elements of modernity. Simply to mention Abelard's name is to bring to mind a few of them, notably an emphasis on scholarship and learning in which one can dimly perceive the first dawning of that seemingly age-old, middle-class tendency to view education as the key to advancement. Schooling was peculiarly an urban phenomenon, and little wonder: so involved had the bourgeoisie become in international commerce and industry that no merchant could hope to survive long unless he had the literacy to handle a far-flung correspondence and the arithmetic to add up accounts. Unlike the nobles, a high proportion of tradesmen could read.

And education did not end with departure from school. Towns and fairs provided a meeting ground for wanderers from all over the known world, and in their encounters took place an exchange of ideas and of cultural values that helped to break down the barriers that centuries of rural insularity had firmly erected. Under Charlemagne, for example, men displayed little interest in Islam and generally regarded Mohammed as having been the Antichrist of the Apocalypse. By the eleventh century, knowledge had unquestionably increased, thanks largely to the start of the Crusades and the reconquest of Spain, but attitudes remained narrow and prejudiced. Knowing that Muslims abstained from both spirits and pork, Europeans in the early twelfth century could blithely explain that these practices had arisen from a reverence for the memory of the Prophet himself, who had had the misfortune to be eaten by swine while lying in a drunken stupor.

Toward the end of the century, however, signs of greater understanding appeared. Translations of the Koran and other Islamic writings were becoming freely available, and on the basis on their content, Gerald of Wales could hesitantly assert that if Muslims refused to eat pork, their abstention owed not a little to Jewish precedent, while their avoidance of wine was probably closely related to its injurious effects when imbibed in a hot, desert climate. Although Islam remained an abomination in the eyes of most people, Gerald's rationality and common sense suggest the extent to which the cultural interchange fostered by trade and the towns had made it possible for Europeans to examine with sympathy even those religious tenets they regarded as hateful.

In so far as the essence of education lies in the whole process of child-rearing itself, the very openness of the urban environment tended to have revolutionary and modernizing effects beyond those produced by the simple exchange of differing values. At the millennium, the peasant could emphasize tradition in raising his children, for he knew that their survival as adults would depend almost exclusively on their having mastered the skills he possessed. But the twelfth-century bourgeois could have no such assurance: despite all the oligarchic and monopolistic restrictions of the gilds, opportunities abounded, and the city-dweller had little guarantee that his sons would enter his trade or pursue his profession. Hence, to teach them only the techniques of his craft was to run the risk of denying them other and greater careers. To meet this problem, there emerged a new and typically bourgeois way to bring up the young. No longer was the properly raised child confined to a particular speciality, encouraged merely to know the externals of his father's profession; instead, his education became increasingly internalized, and he was expected automatically to appreciate the importance of inner values and of self-discipline, qualities on which he was taught to rely, regardless of circumstances. Above all, he was trained to think for himself so that he could solve the variety of problems with which his still unknown career would confront him. In short, the bourgeoisie rejected the traditional approach of the peasants and adopted a method whose abstract procedures and principles might better enable the young to cope with the challenge of urban diversity.

These changes had a clear impact on the literature of the period, and nowhere more noticeably than in those *fabliaux* or moral tales for which the bourgeoisie showed such a striking partiality. Frequently Eastern in origin, these stories both reflected the growing cosmopolitanism of the towns and served, when suitably modified for Western tastes, as vehicles for the dissemination of maxims on which a proper inner-directedness could be based. In *The Lay of the Little Bird*, for example, a nameless peasant carle snares a magical lark that he proposes to take from its enchanted garden and cage for its song. The bird, however, persuades him to set it free, promising to teach him three secrets. Yet when he agrees and the bird is safely perched at the top of a pine-tree, the first turns out to be: '*Yield not a ready faith to every tale*'. Upon protesting this trickery, the peasant then receives the second: '*What's lost, 'tis wise with patience to forego*'. Lastly comes the third, and with it the conclusion of the lay:

> 'Peace,' quoth the bird; 'my third is far the best;
> Store thou the precious treasure in thy breast:
> *What good thou hast, ne'er lightly from thee cast.*'
> He spoke, and twittering fled away full fast.
> Straight, sunk in earth, the gushing fountain dries;
> Down fall the fruits; the withered pine-tree dies;
> Fades all the beauteous plat, so cool, so green,
> Into thin air, and never more is seen.
>   Such was the meed of avarice: – bitter cost!
> The carle, who all would gather, all had lost.[50]

If, for all its charm, this tale has about it a certain air of *déja vu* banality, it is largely because the virtues it propounds have continued to form the foundations of the sensible, middle-class outlook. Nonetheless, familiarity with the point of view should not be allowed to obscure the fact that in the twelfth century the inner-directedness of *The Lay of the Little Bird* had revolutionary implications. Men who were not bound by tradition became thereby more open to change, and insofar as inventiveness was prized by a class whose very training had led it to be ambitious, the consequence was a society in which progress could be more readily achieved.

And while it is true that a marked cautiousness, even stodginess, pervades the maxims of the *fabliaux*, no one should be misled into believing that the bourgeoisie had already fallen into the stereotypes of its modern detractors, for in practice the merchants and tradesmen of the towns were much too full of life and vitality to be restrained by the moralism of their literature. Perhaps William Fitz-Stephen best captured the essence of the urban ideal when he remarked that 'a city should not only be commodious and serious, but also merry and sportful'. If so, then it is in his descriptions of the diversions of the bourgeois of London that the true atmosphere of the age may be found:

But London ... hath holy plays, representations of miracles which holy confessors have wrought, or representations of the torments wherein the constancy of martyrs appeared. Every year also at Shrove Tuesday ... the schoolboys do bring cocks of the game to their master, and all the forenoon they delight themselves in cock-fighting: after dinner, all the youths go into the fields to play at the ball. . .

In Easter holidays they fight battles on the water: a shield is hung upon a pole, fixed in the midst of the stream, a boat is prepared without oars, to be carried by violence of the water, and in the fore part thereof standeth a young man, ready to give charge upon the shield with his lance; if so be he breaketh his lance against the shield and doth not fall, he is thought to have performed a worthy deed; if so be, without breaking his lance, he runneth strongly against the shield, down he falleth into the water, for the boat is violently forced with the tide; but on each side of the shield ride two boats, furnished with young men, which recover him that falleth as soon as they may. Upon the bridge, wharfs, and houses, by the river's side, stand great numbers to see and laugh thereat. . . . In winter, every holiday before dinner, the boats prepared for brawn are set to fight, or else bulls and bears are baited.

When the great fen, or moor, which watereth the walls of the city on the north side, is frozen, many young men play upon the ice; . . . some tie bones to their feet and under their heels; and shoving themselves by a little picked staff, do slide as swiftly as a bird flieth in the air, or an arrow out of a crossbow. . . . Many of the citizens do delight themselves in hawks and hounds: for they have liberty of hunting in Middlesex, Hertfordshire, all Chiltern, and in Kent to the water of Cray.[51]

Such, then, were some of the pleasures of the city, and with them one returns to that boisterous sense of enthusiasm with which Fulcher of Chartres first beheld the wonders of Constantinople. And though urban life was not without its blemishes, it is here that the chapter should end, for to do otherwise would be only to distort the picture and do injustice to all that was best in medieval man.

6 The Upper Orders and the Crusading Ideal

For many people, the Crusades conjure up scenes of incredible romance, scenes in which the Age of Faith appears on the march, pennons unfurled and armour sparkling in the sun. The army itself is made up of noble men, ferocious and warlike, perhaps, but gentled by a proud chivalry to which the cross on each shoulder gives visible witness. In all history there are few events that have stirred the popular imagination as much as the Crusades.

The romantic view is not entirely mistaken, for many incidents sustain it. There is, for example, the tumultuous conclave at Clermont in 1095 where Urban II's appeal was so overwhelmingly met with cries of 'God wills it! God wills it!' and the decision to create a crusading force that soon carried an exiled pope back to Rome and the Christians themselves to the Holy Land and eventual victory at Jerusalem. Then, too, one thinks of the visionary Peter the Hermit, whose preaching to the common people kindled a response beyond all rational comprehension. Or of the unexpected humility of proud Godfrey of Bouillon, a man who turned down the crown of the Latin Kingdom of Jerusalem, preferring to be called merely the Defender of the Holy Sepulchre because he refused to wear gold where his Saviour had been forced to wear thorns. Moreover, there is the romance of the Third Crusade with its stories of Richard the Lion-Hearted to whom Saladin sent cooling ices from the mountains when he lay ill in his tent before the walls of Jaffa. Lastly, there emerges the endless tragedy, notably of Richard himself, a warrior who failed to recapture Jerusalem, and who refused to visit it as a pilgrim because, as Richard of Devizes reported it, 'the worthy indignation of his noble mind could not consent to receive that from the courtesy of the Gentiles which he could not obtain by the gift of God'.[52]

On the other hand, the Crusades had a darker, less edifying side, one whose obvious greed has led some critics to see in them little more than the first appearance of that modern imperialism which so piously took up the White Man's Burden – but only at a profit. Anna Comnena, daughter of the Byzantine emperor who first appealed to Urban II for aid, protested that 'the Latin race is always very fond of money, but more especially when it is bent on raiding a country; it then loses its reason and gets beyond control'.[53] And that her observations were justified is suggested by a letter of Count Stephen of Blois, who found it possible on the road to the Holy Land to write reassuringly to his wife: 'You may know for certain, my beloved, that of gold, silver and many other kind of riches I now have twice as much as your love had assigned to me when I left you'.[54] Similarly, these expeditions often appeared singularly lacking in that chivalry which a romantic idealism so easily ascribes to them. On the fall of Jerusalem in 1099, Raymond of St Gilles, count of Toulouse, calmly informed the pope: 'And if you desire to know what was done with the enemy who were found there, know that in Solomon's Porch and in his temple our men rode in the blood of the Saracens up to the knees of their horses'.[55] The Fourth Crusade failed to reach the Holy Land, but sacked Constantinople instead, while the Sixth was led by a man so abominable, Frederick II, that the pope found it necessary to excommunicate both him and his descendants to all eternity. As for those Crusades that a militant papacy turned against the heretics of Europe, perhaps all that needs to be known is that when the papal legate was queried about the fate of the inhabitants of Béziers, a town that fell to the Albigensian crusaders in 1209, he is supposed to have replied: 'Kill them all. God will recognize His own'. Though the remark is doubtless apocryphal, its import proved terribly real, for thousands were massacred in the ensuing slaughter.

Even relations among the crusaders themselves were not without conflicts and jealousies, and if the leaders of the First Crusade were able to resolve their petty disputes, the quarrels of Richard the Lion-Hearted, Philip Augustus of France and Duke Leopold of Austria became notorious on the Third. Each refused to fight for the others, and on returning to Europe, Leopold went so far as to seize Richard and hold him to ransom. Philip, not to be outdone, took advantage of this opportunity to begin the reconquest of Normandy, all the while promising the emperor and the Austrians a generous subsidy for every day they could prolong the Lion-Heart's captivity.

And rivalries were not confined to the leadership. Supposedly warriors of God, all fighting only in His service, the crusaders were in fact quick to export their national jealousies and continue their feuds even on the land where their Saviour had trod. Frenchmen hated Germans; Englishmen hated French. The result was endless recrimination, as reflected in Geoffrey de Vinsauf's very English account of the hopeless depravity of Philip Augustus' fun-loving French:

The very men who were supposed to have been led by their devotion to succour the Holy Land now left the camp and abandoned themselves to amatory and effeminate songs and debaucheries, for, as was told by those who saw them, they delighted in dancing-women; and their luxurious apparel bespoke their effeminacy, for the sleeves of their garments were fastened with gold chains, and they wantonly exposed their waists, which were confined with embroidered belts; ...

and around their necks they wore collars glittering with jewels, and on their heads garlands interwoven with flowers of every hue; they carried goblets, not swords, in their hands, and after spending whole nights in drinking and carousing, they went heated with wine to the houses of prostitutes, and if by chance they were preoccupied, and the door was closed against them, they pulled it down, giving utterance to language and oaths which horrified those who heard them, as is well known from the habits of the French. In a word, their external condition proved their inward levity. Shame on the French for indulging in such excesses![56]

With stories like this in circulation, it seems hardly surprising, that Usāmah, a Muslim contemporary of Saladin, should have incredulously exclaimed:

Mysterious are the works of the Creator, the author of all things! When one comes to recount cases regarding the Franks, he cannot but glorify Allah (exalted is he!) and sanctify him, for he sees them as animals possessing the virtues of courage and fighting, but nothing else. . . .[57]

A low estimate, perhaps – and yet more than Geoffrey de Vinsauf was willing to admit for the French.

Be that as it may, these examples serve to suggest that the Crusades present a certain problem in historical interpretation. With them, as with so much in medieval life, the modern observer confronts a strange mixture of piety and savagery whose striking contrasts would seemingly defy all efforts to understand them. In fact, however, the answer is not very far to seek, and it does much to explain how the untamed aristocracy of the millennium was gradually transformed into a nobility that was both more refined in its tastes and better prepared to accept the dictates of a chivalrous ethic.

For the warriors of Europe, the eleventh century proved a time of rapid change, most of it inimical to their traditional interests. Although fighting hardly abated, warfare tended to take on quite different goals. The battles of the ninth and tenth century had resulted in anarchy and decentralization, in a devolution of authority that followed naturally from the inability of those in control to resist successfully the ambitions of their vassals. After 1000, however, the tide began to turn, and the struggles of the eleventh century increasingly centred on the extent to which counts and dukes would be able to re-establish some semblance of order in their principalities. Given prevailing conditions, the recognition of extensive territorial authority was not easily obtained. Fulk Nerra the Black, who became count of Anjou in 987, was more talented than most, but it still took the greater part of his long reign to subjugate most of his county; and when, in 1040, he died on a pilgrimage to Jerusalem, his son Geoffrey Martel soon discovered that, for all his father's efforts, much remained to be done. Nor was the experience of other regions notably different. The counts of Flanders spent much of their time subduing recalcitrant castellans, while in Normandy the attempts of Duke Richard II to consolidate his power collapsed within months of his death. In the following year, 1027, his son Richard III was murdered, and when Robert I failed to return from *his* pilgrimage to the Holy Land in 1035, the scene was set for William the Conqueror's bloody minority, twelve years of chaos in which the young duke saw friends, relatives and tutors alike consigned to a violent doom. Only in 1047, with William's victory at Val ès Dunes – and really not until 1060 – can it be said that ducal authority fully prevailed.

Nevertheless, arduous as the task proved to be, order was slowly restored. By the second half of the century, many areas of Europe enjoyed a modicum of peace, free from the devastation of petty disputes and private warfare. In some instances, respect for authority was imposed by force; in others, skilled diplomacy and shrewd marriage alliances seemed all that was necessary. In every case, however, better instruments of government were created and the continuing power of the regime was ensured through the construction of new castles, for the first time erected in stone, over which each ruler was careful to maintain an inflexible control.

In practical terms, the emergence of viable territorial principalities meant nothing less than the imposition of discipline on a fighting class for which any form of restraint had previously been anathema. And it is here, possibly, that the genius of William the Conqueror shines forth most brightly, for the invasion of England could never have been carried out if he had not had a singular ability to organize and command a heterogeneous body of men. His was a remarkable achievement, and something of its excitement comes through in William of Poitiers' account of the preparations preceding the Conquest:

It would be tedious to tell in detail how by his prudent acts ships were made, arms and troops, provisions and other equipment assembled for war, and how the enthusiasm of the whole of Normandy was directed towards this enterprise. Nor did he neglect to take measures for the administration and the security of the duchy during his absence. Further, many warriors came to his support from outside the duchy, some being attracted by his well-known generosity, and all by confidence in the justice of his cause. Such was his moderation and prudence that he utterly forbade pillage, and provided for fifty thousand soldiers at his own cost for a whole month while contrary winds delayed them at the mouth of the Dives. He made generous provision both for his own knights and those from other parts, but he did not allow any of them to take their sustenance by force. The flocks and herds of the peasantry pastured unharmed throughout the province. The crops waited undisturbed for the sickle without being tramped by the pride of knights or ravaged by the greed of the plunderer. A weak and unarmed man, watching the swarm of soldiers without fear, might follow his horse singing wherever he would.[58]

Exaggerated though William of Poitiers' narration may be, it makes clear that men like William the Conqueror would brook none of the excesses that had hitherto formed the greater part of the aristocracy's recreational activities.

Nor were secular leaders alone in their disciplinary endeavours, for the eleventh-century Church, increasingly reformed, was equally anxious to put an end to the feuds and private warfare that threatened to tear European society apart. Indeed, the re-establishment of an enduring peace was soon to become one of the practical aims of the reform itself.

Needless to say, the Church had initially had few such ambitions. The monasteries of the Cluniac movement displayed little interest in changing the world; their concerns were almost exclusively sacramental and monkish. Moreover, in so far as monastic reform depended, at least in its early stages, on a close cooperation with the secular aristocracy, it seems doubtful whether many of its leaders would ever have thought to challenge the customs and habits of those on whose assistance they relied. In the eleventh century, however, there came a change in mood: just as the Blacks in contemporary America have tended to turn on the White Liberals to whom they had originally appealed for support, so too the most militant of the clerical reformers turned on the laity, arguing that the Church could never be cleansed of its faults until it had completely renounced all ties with the world. Further, they held that the Church belonged solely to its priests and that its purification required nothing less than the total rejection of all secular interference in the management of its affairs, notably in the appointment of bishops and abbots.

In its most familiar form, this militancy led to the Investiture Conflict, a complex and confusing struggle that first broke out in 1075 when Gregory VII forbade prelates to receive their symbols of office from the hands of a layman. In this guise, it caused the political disintegration of Germany, the exiling of St Anselm from the see of Canterbury and, indirectly, even the martyrdom of Becket. But, most important of all, it established a papal primacy in both secular and religious affairs that was to last for centuries.

The peace movement arose in this context. Discernible as early as the decade preceding the millennium, when a few bishops began attempting to restrain the warlike activities of their flocks, it then gathered momentum and rapidly grew during the course of the following century. Initially, its successes were modest. By alleging the impropriety of combat on the days of the Lord's crucifixion and resurrection, a cleric might temporarily persuade his parishioners to abstain from fighting on Fridays and Sundays, but any proposal to enlarge the scope of these truces was likely to end in defeat. Even within the Church itself it proved remarkably difficult to tame the ferocity of the clergy. When, for example, provincial synods made it a point of canon law that no priest should shed blood, some prelates were quick to adopt the mace, a weapon that could crush an enemy's skull without shedding a drop of it. Others refused to change their ways at all, and if William the Conqueror was the victor at Hastings, the Bayeux Tapestry makes it apparent that his success owed not a little to the club and right arm of his half-brother Odo, the bishop of Bayeux.

Yet, despite a multitude of failures, the peace movement gradually developed a number of techniques that proved more effective. Of these, by far the most important was the so-called diocesan association, an organization of episcopal creation that for the first time provided some measure of protection against the outbreak of private war. Its methods were simple in the extreme. The bishop would call together all males of fifteen or older in his diocese and then make them swear that none would break the peace, the terms of which were carefully specified. Anyone failing to observe this oath was subject to immediate excommunication, and the rest of the membership was expected to form a diocesan army which, under the leadership of the bishop, would attempt to bring the wrongdoer to justice. In this way a 'peace of God' was established.

Although the results obtained were far from perfect, these diocesan associations had many advantages over other and looser arrangements. Because all were involved in the oath, none could escape from its obligations; moreover, the sanctions provided were very real. Few men in the eleventh century found it possible to contemplate the threat of excommunication with equanimity; the sacraments were much too important to be lightly abandoned. And, even assuming that a man was willing thus to endanger his immortal soul, he still had to face the likelihood of being physically overwhelmed by the forces of the diocesan army. In short, a person wishing to engage in private warfare often found the price not worth paying, and that the peace associations proved their worth is possibly nowhere better illustrated than in the fact that they were to become the model for the organization of urban communes. It must be added, however, that the ultimate success of the peace movement was not entirely the product of its own endeavours. Rather, in the course of the century it was joined in its efforts by the rulers of the territorial principalities, men hardly blind to the advantages that a stable peace could afford them. Thus in Normandy, the peace of God was transformed into the duke's peace, and the man foolhardy enough to tempt fate in battle quickly discovered that he was answerable for his actions not only to God and a diocesan army, but also to the avenging wrath of William the Conqueror himself. It was not a pleasant prospect.

By the end of the eleventh century, the aristocracy found itself in an exceedingly uncomfortable position. From earliest youth its members had been trained to do nothing but fight, and few of them could even begin to conceive of any other life. On the other hand, their warfare was greeted by open hostility on the part of the one institution, the Church, for which they showed the slightest respect. Few nobles understood the faith into which they had been baptized, and fewer still had the discipline to live by its tenets. For most, religious duty entailed little more than the occasional reception of the sacraments, a modicum of penance for their frequent misdeeds, and constant veneration of relics, those physical vestiges of the saintly that were taken as concrete proofs of the divine. Of greater heights their minds were incapable.

Yet, like the peasants and clergy, the nobles believed in Christianity from the depths of their being. Religion gave meaning to their lives, for it was only in the promise of a better world to come that they found the strength to endure the senseless conflicts that marked their daily existence. Raised to fight but wanting salvation, the nobility understandably viewed the spread of the peace of God as nothing short of catastrophic. To accept it was to deny the whole of the warrior's raison d'être while to defy it was to risk losing that eternity with God for which all men yearned. It seemed an impossible dilemma.

Such was the atmosphere prevailing in Europe when Urban II chose to preach his Crusade. It was a masterful performance, and even though his exact words were never recorded, every version makes clear the nature of their greatness. In Fulcher of Chartres' account, Urban opened mildly, addressing his listeners as 'the salt of the earth' and as 'sons of God'. But his mood changed when he came to speak of civil disorder:

Whoever lays violent hands on a bishop, let him be considered excommunicated. Whoever shall have seized monks, or priests, or nuns, and their servants, or pilgrims, or traders, and shall have despoiled them, let him be accursed. Let thieves and burners of houses and their accomplices be excommunicated from the church and accursed. . . .

By these evils, therefore, as I have said, dearest breathren, you have seen the world disordered for a long time, and to such a degree that in some places in your provinces, as has been reported to us . . . , one scarcely dares to travel for fear of being kidnapped by thieves at night or highwaymen by day, by force or by craft, at home or out of doors.[59]

Under threat of anathema, the pope then enjoined his bishops to enforce the peace and truce of God, and with Europe thus disposed of, he turned to the plight of the Holy Land. Perhaps Robert the Monk's version is most faithful:

From the confines of Jerusalem and the city of Constantinople a horrible tale has gone forth and very frequently has been brought to our ears: namely, that a race from the kingdom of the Persians, an accursed race, a race utterly alienated from God, a generation, forsooth, which has neither directed its heart nor entrusted its spirit to God, has invaded the lands of those Christians and has depopulated them by the sword, pillage and fire. . . . They destroy the altars, after having defiled them with their uncleanness. They circumcise the Christians, and the blood of the circumcision they either spread upon the altars or pour into the vases of the baptismal font. When they wish to torture people by a base death, they perforate their navels, and, dragging forth the end of the intestines, bind it to a stake: then with flogging they lead the victim around until his viscera have gushed forth, and he falls prostrate upon the ground. Others they bind to a post and pierce with arrows. Others they compel to extend their necks, and then, attacking them with naked swords, they attempt to cut through the neck with a single blow. What shall I say of the abominable rape of women? To speak of it is worse than to be silent. ... Let the Holy Sepulchre of the Lord, our Saviour, which is possessed by un-clean nations, especially move you, and likewise the holy places, which are now treated with ignominy and irreverently polluted with filthiness.[60]

Having renewed the prohibition of warfare in Europe, and having vividly described the desecration of God's holy places in terms well calculated to raise the blood-lust of his beholders, Urban was at last ready for his perora-tion. The version of Fulcher of Chartres is best:

Wherefore, I exhort with earnest prayer – not I, but God – that, as heralds of Christ, you urge men by frequent exhortation, men of all ranks, knights as well as foot-soldiers, rich as well as poor, to hasten to exterminate this vile race from the lands of your brethren, and to aid the Christians in time. I speak to those present; I proclaim it to the absent; moreover, Christ commands it. And if those who set out thither should lose their lives on the way by land, or in crossing the sea, or in fighting the pagans, their sins shall be remitted. This I grant to all who go, through the power vested in me by God. Oh, what a disgrace, if a race so despised, base, and the instrument of demons, should so overcome a people endowed with faith in the all-powerful God, and resplendent with the name of Christ! Oh, what re-proaches will be charged against you by the Lord Himself if you have not helped those who are counted, like yourselves, of the Christian faith! Let those who have been accustomed to make private war against the faithful carry on to a successful issue a war against infidels, which ought to have begun ere now. Let those who for a long time have been robbers now become soldiers of Christ. Let those who once fought against brothers and relatives now fight against barbarians, as they ought. ... Let no obstacle stand in the way of those who are going, but ... let them zealously undertake the journey under the guidance of the Lord.[61]

A better speech would be hard to imagine, so perfectly was it attuned to the mood of the times. For Urban well knew that in crusading he was offering a program that would rid the nobility of most of the difficulties that the imposition of the peace of God had entailed. In driving the infidels from the Holy Land, warriors would be able to engage freely in the one occupation for which they had been trained; ambitions of a lifetime could be fulfilled without incurring the danger of eternal damnation, for to fight was now no more than to do the Church's bidding. Training and religion were thus combined, thereby ensuring an expedition of unparalled barbarity. In capturing Jerusalem men would ride 'in the blood of the Saracens up to the knees of their horses', but far from fearing for their immortal souls because of this carnage, they would immediately repair to the Church of the Holy Sepulchre where, with a *Te Deum*, they could give thanks for it.

Moreover, in preaching his Crusade, Urban II was making an appeal that spoke to the faith of the age. Poorly as the nobles might understand the complexities of their religion, they could readily comprehend the importance of the Holy Land. From the end of the tenth century its shrines had begun to attract European pilgrims and, hazardous though everyone knew the journey to be, men as brutal and violent as Fulk Nerra of Anjou and Robert of Normandy had nevertheless proved willing to lay down their lives just for the opportunity of making it. To mentalities such as theirs, death was a small price to pay, for in the popular mind the Holy Land had taken on a significance more usually associated with the veneration of relics. Its very concreteness made its meaning easy to grasp and, because the Saviour Himself had lived there, finally suffering crucifixion so that others might live, as a relic it seemed uncommonly precious.

Small wonder, then, that hundreds of thousands should have responded to Urban's appeal. To visit the Holy Places – or to recapture them, now that they appeared so shamefully defiled – was to gain visible proof of God's existence, and merely to see the earthly Jerusalem was to catch a glimpse of that heavenly city toward which all men strove. Some would not reach this goal, but even to those unfortunate enough to fall along the way Urban could promise remission of sins, thereby blunting the fear of death and replacing it with the hope of salvation. Seldom in history has a speech been better conceived for its audience, and seldom has one had greater consequences.

In a sense, though, the consequences did not involve crusading itself, a movement that ended in ultimate failure. Rather, the true importance of the Crusades lay in the forces they generated, forces that had an incalculable effect on every aspect of European life. To the reformed Church, the universal enthusiasm that greeted the papal speech at Clermont meant that reform itself had been largely accepted. No more did Rome slumber amidst decay and corruption; she was again mistress of the world, and it would be hundreds of years before anyone would successfully challenge her dominion. Even further, the Church's leaders developed a new sense of mission, and they became determined to root out every vestige of former degradation. St Bernard, himself the sponsor of the Second Crusade, could view only with scorn the luxurious sacramentalism of Cluny, not to mention the waywardness of its monks. Though the Cluniacs had remained true to the ideals which had first given them being, the abbot of Clairvaux was quick to point out that times had changed:

I marvel how monks could grow accustomed to such intemperance in eating and drinking, clothing and bedding, riding abroad and building, that, wheresoever these things are wrought most busily and with most pleasure and expense, there Religion is thought to be best kept. For behold! spare living is taken for covetousness, sobriety for austerity, silence for melancholy; while, on the other hand, men rebaptize laxity as 'discretion', waste as 'liberality', garrulousness as 'affability', giggling as 'jollity', effeminacy in clothing and bedding as 'neatness'.... I say naught of the vast height of your churches, their immoderate length, their superfluous breadth, the costly polishings, the curious carvings and paintings which attract the worshipper's gaze and hinder his attention, and seem to me in some sort a revival of the ancient Jewish rites. Let this pass, however: say that this is done for God's honour.[62]

For better or worse, the day of the Cluniacs was passing; the twelfth century had discovered other ideals, notably those of Cîteaux. Withdrawn from the world and practising a rigid austerity almost puritanical in its zeal, the Cistercians displayed all the ardour characteristic of a new order. St Bernard was their spokesman, and with thousands seeking to join their ranks, they rapidly assumed a pre-eminent place in the religious affairs of Europe. Not even the papacy itself could escape from their militant criticism, and in the emotional fire of their rhetoric one senses the extent of their debt to the all-pervasive influence of the crusading ideal. Here, for example, is Bernard attempting to coax the return of a monk who had abandoned his calling:

Arise, soldier of Christ, arise, shake off the dust, return to the battle whence thou hast fled, and more bravely shalt thou fight and more gloriously triumph. Christ has many soldiers who bravely began, stood fast and conquered: He has few who have turned from flight and renewed the combat. Everything rare is precious; and thou among that rare company shalt the more radiantly shine.

Thou art fearful? so be it; but why dost thou fear where there is no fear, and why dost thou not fear where everything is to be feared?... Dost thou recoil at the weight of thy arms, O delicate soldier! Before the enemy's darts the shield is no burden, nor the helmet heavy. The bravest soldiers tremble when the trumpet is heard before the battle is joined; but then hope of victory and fear of defeat make them brave. How canst thou tremble, walled round with the zeal of thy armed brethren, angels bearing aid at thy right hand, and thy leader Christ? There shalt thou safely fight, secure of victory. O battle, safe with Christ and for Christ![63]

Yet, in spite of a rhetoric that could dwell on the joys of the fray, St Bernard's writings were more frequently filled with thoughts of love. In this he was typical of his age. Like most of his contemporaries, he rejected a theology of wrath, replacing it with a vision of an omnipotent Deity whose loving concern had not only created the world, but would also redeem it. For Bernard, love had a mystical significance, and he was to spend years in trying to explain how a love of self for self's sake could be upraised and transformed into a love of Divinity so intense that even self would ultimately be loved only for the sake of God. And though he doubted whether such ecstasy were attainable in this life, he remained confident that it would prove the essence of the next.

Few theologians went this far in their speculations, but most joined the abbot of Clairvaux in emphasizing the example of love so readily apparent in the Holy Family itself. Here again the Crusades betray their influence;

indeed, the extent to which Jesus, Mary and Joseph became central to all doctrines of love leads one to suspect that this whole development might never have taken place had it not been for the struggles then raging beyond the sea. But because they were, and because every man's gaze was drawn to events in the Holy Land, it was natural that thinkers should have begun to consider the meaning and purpose of the lives of those whose shrines the crusaders sought to recover. St Anselm explored the mystery of the Incarnation, demonstrating the abundance of God's love which alone could explain it; St Bernard himself was nowhere more moving than in his discussions of Mary and her Child. Even the cathedrals of the age reflected similar interests, for, whether Romanesque or early Gothic in style, they were often dedicated in the name of the Virgin while, contrary to previous tendencies, their sculptural ornamentation showed a distinct preference for scenes from the Nativity, not the Last Judgment. The whole of Christ's life became an object of intense contemplation, and in summing up the doctrine of love, Bernard made it clear that all could profit from His example:

> He loved sweetly, wisely, and bravely: sweetly, in that He put on flesh; wisely, in that He avoided fault; bravely, in that He bore death. Those, however, with whom He sojourned in the flesh, He did not love carnally, but in prudence of spirit. Learn then, Christian, from Christ how to love. . . .[64]

Although the laity never fully accepted this saintly advice, the outlook of the twelfth-century nobility changed, and in ways that parallelled developments in the Church. If the knight of earlier times had been purely the warrior, with religious convictions bearing little relation to the profession he followed, under the impact of the Crusades these two sides of his personality began to merge. During the eleventh century the nobility had been brought to heel both by the peace of God and the growing power of territorial princes; forbidden to fight unless its cause were just, it had then been turned loose to slaughter the infidel for the greater glory of God. Suddenly transformed into soldiers of Christ, most nobles increasingly assumed that the bearing of arms was to be viewed as a religious experience. Hence it was that the ceremonies surrounding initiation to knighthood took on aspects of a sacramental rite, with candidates expected to pray for divine guidance the whole of the night preceding their dubbing. Priests bestowed blessings on men and arms alike; sermons were preached on the nature of knightly virtue; martial training itself came to include an emphasis on certain standards of conduct that were soon to be regularized in a series of precise, if idealized, codes. In a word, the age of chivalry had arrived.

Yet, much as this new ethic owed to the Crusades, it owed an equal debt to other factors. The true knight may have imagined himself caparisoned in the garb of a crusader, but if the nobility was required to refrain from rapine and pillage while simultaneously protecting the rights of widows and orphans,

Knighthood in Flower

Even in the stained glass of an Essex church, the mounted knight ruled supreme.

Heavy mail was often a nuisance but when Lancelot rescued Guinevere (*below*) he found an unexpected use for his sword.

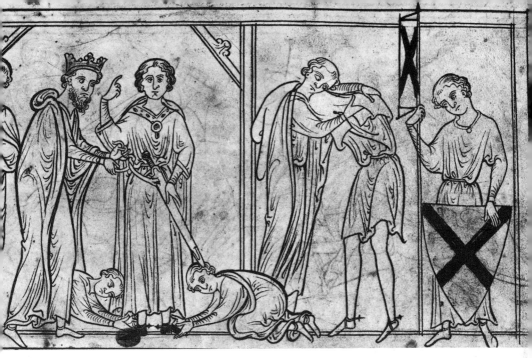

Squires longed for the
day when they too
would be dubbed
knights (*above*).
Crusaders paid homage
primarily to God
(*right*).

At Chartres, even the confessor saints became ideal warriors (*left*).

Below : ivory chessmen (knights) from the Island of Lewis.

Sir Geoffrey Luttrell takes leave of his wife and daughter-in-law (*above*); knights and ladies ride out to a tournament (*below*).

In courtly romance the knight received every attention (*left*) – but the delights of love were not without their limitations (*above*, 'The triumph of love' (tempera), mid-fifteenth century, Florentine).

Joan of Arc drove all doubtful companions from the army. Even in the one known contemporaneous sketch (*left*), she looks a very determined woman.

it was hardly because this policy had ever been followed with regard to infidels. Far from it. Rather, its origins lay in the specific prohibitions embodied in those eleventh-century peace associations to which all men had been forced to adhere, often against their deeper instincts. Moreover, if the twelfth-century nobility proved willing to accept, at least as an ideal, a set of regulations that its ancestors had not, much of the new attitude reflected a growing awareness of class and self-interest. With the rise of the towns, nobles were no longer the sole possessors of wealth, and as they watched the successes of the bourgeoisie, they were moved to close ranks and emphasize all those qualities which made their position unique. In their view, they alone deserved the leadership of society, for they alone possessed the fighting abilities needed to preserve peace and security. Further, unlike the bourgeoisie, most of whose members had arisen from obscure origins, the nobility could claim considerable pride of ancestry, a point it was quick to stress both by creating mythical genealogies stretching back to the Trojans and by introducing coats of arms to which no *nouveau-riche* merchant could hope to aspire. It mattered little that these armorial devices seem actually to have been invented to aid in the indentification of knights whose faces were being increasingly shrouded by ever more cumbersome helmets; if these blazons were useful in combating bourgeois pretensions, then they would be so employed. And, in much the same way, if the nobles came to accept most of the tenets of chivalry, it was partly because they thought that chivalrous behaviour would help them maintain their aristocratic superiority.

It seems doubtful, however, whether many nobles fully appreciated the extent to which they were becoming tamed and civilized. For the process was slow, and in some measure it represented nothing more than a grudging recognition on the part of the warlike that they could never escape from the discipline to which they were relentlessly subjected. Certainly there were still to be enough outcroppings of violence and terror to prove that the penchant for brutality was far from ended. Yet, even as some continued to glory in battle, others displayed signs of a different attitude, one in which the powers of the mind were increasingly employed to bridle the unthinking passion of the emotions.

We know, for example, that it was during this period that chess first began to be popular among the upper classes. Though a game of war, something which doubtless helped to increase its appeal, above all else it is a thinking man's game, hardly suited to the abilities of the impetuous: few people in the tenth century could ever have hoped to attempt it. Similarly, a possible preference for thought and restraint is to be found even in *The Song of Roland*. Roland may in every way be the fighting hero, much to be admired, but as the story proceeds, the poet points out that he lacks at least one of Oliver's virtues: 'Roland is brave. His friend is brave – and wise'.[65] This difference creates tension, for though Oliver three times implores Roland to summon aid, the latter refuses, arguing that to follow this advice would be to bring dishonour. Thus, when Roland finally changes his mind, Oliver's anger is great:

> And Roland cried: 'Why are you wroth with me?'
> The other answered: 'Comrade, all the fault
> Is yours. To temper knightlihood with sense
> Is not unknightly: valor must be joined
> With measure. Through your foolish arrogance
> The Franks are dead, and nevermore will fight
> For Charles. If you had given heed, the King
> Would now be here. We should have fought and won.'[66]

The *chansons de geste* were not the only form of literature seeking to moderate the passions of the nobility; the twelfth century was more an age of courtly romance, and in its tales of Arthurian round tables, unfulfilled love and quests for the grail, one theme was constantly re-echoed: that pursuit of the grail or of one's lady was greatly preferable to pursuit of one's enemy; indeed, that hate for one's enemy was to be subordinated to religious or secular love.

To the nobility, this doctrine of love was no less novel than St Bernard's had been to the clergy, and toward the end of the century the task of explaining its meaning fell to Andreas Capellanus:

Love is a certain inborn suffering derived from the sight of and excessive meditation upon the beauty of the opposite sex, which causes each one to wish above all things the embraces of the other and by common desire to carry out all of love's precepts in the other's embrace.[67]

Further, for those uncertain as to whether they were truly in love, Andreas thoughtfully provided a series of rules:

1 Marriage is no real excuse for not loving.
2 He who is not jealous cannot love. . . .
4 It is well known that love is always increasing or decreasing.
5 That which a lover takes against the will of his beloved has no relish. . . .
12 A true lover does not desire to embrace in love anyone except his beloved.
13 When made public love rarely endures.
14 The easy attainment of love makes it of little value; difficulty of attainment makes it prized.
15 Every lover regularly turns pale in the presence of his beloved.
16 When a lover suddenly catches sight of his beloved his heart palpitates. . . .
21 Real jealousy always increases the feeling of love. . . .
25 A true lover considers nothing good except what he thinks will please his beloved. . . .
27 A lover can never have enough of the solaces of his beloved. . . .[68]

In such rules, foolish though they often appear, are to be found the roots of that romantic love which was for so long to dominate all Western thinking on the subject. And though the origins of courtly romance have themselves provoked endless dispute, they sprang primarily from that same source which produced not only chivalry, but clerical doctrines of love. For the influence of the Crusades was pervasive. With husbands far distant in the Holy Land, wives became the patrons of literature, and since they responded most eagerly to tales stressing the worth and desirability of women, troubadours naturally hastened to meet their demands. Moreover, returning crusaders proved more willing to accept these feminine tastes than might have been expected. As soldiers of Christ, they found kinship with the knights of the round table, and in the quest for the grail they could discern a romantic projection of their own adventures. Indeed, in so far as their wanderings had exposed them to the compelling majesty of Mary, not to mention the sinuous delights of Arabic erotica, they were even prepared to elevate the status of women and to hear all of their virtues proclaimed.

Courtly literature did much to refine the tastes of the nobility by introducing it to a world of manners and restraint. In matters of love, unbridled passion was hardly desirable, and in the etiquette of romance many nobles discovered an emotional outlet that was far more agreeable than the agonized brutality of war. Further, to the extent that courtly literature relied on adulterous themes, it provided a vehicle through which many could sublimate the frustrations to which their loveless marriages of convenience so frequently led.

By the end of the twelfth century, then, nobility and clergy alike had come a long way from the turbulent rabble that had first responded to Urban II's crusading appeal. With the appearance of chivalry and love, Europe had arrived at a new level of civilization, one possessing a cultural coherence unknown since the fall of Rome. No longer could developments in one sphere of activity go unnoticed in others, and no more would the continent be dominated by men who saw no relationship between their religious and secular values. Men had at last reunited the fragmented elements of their society, and the buoyant enthusiasm to which this accomplishment inevitably gave rise came to prevail in all classes. No one expressed it more simply, perhaps, than that unknown Goliard poet for whom the rediscovered joys of nature were such a remarkable boon:

> Spring returns, the long awaited,
> Laugh, be glad!

Part 3

The Apogee
1180-1300

7 The Thirteenth-century Synthesis

Although Europe's cultural inheritance began to take on unity and coherence during the twelfth century, the process was only later completed. The peace movement and the Crusades had done much to harmonize the goals of nobility and clergy, but until the thirteenth century society as a whole continued to be shot through with tensions and conflict. Then, however, a genuine synthesis emerged. In France, for example, the rapacity of lords such as Fulk Nerra of Anjou gave way to the moderate rule of Louis IX, a monarch whose reputation for piety and justice was to bring him sainthood within a generation of his death; in England, where kings were less holy, men could still find comfort in the granting of Magna Carta, the first summonses to Parliament, and the increasing codification of common law, all steps that helped to create a constitutional framework for the more peaceful settlement of political and social disputes.

More importantly, the thirteenth-century synthesis momentarily resolved the obvious conflict between religious and secular values. Ever since Constantine's acceptance of Christianity, many of the devout had practised monastic withdrawal, arguing that the world was no more than a sad vale of tears, filled with the snares and temptations of the devil. Nevertheless, by the opening of the thirteenth century, it seemed so no longer: St Francis of Assisi would gladly abandon the life of seclusion and, glorying in the beauties of God's creation, he would preach even to the little birds. For him, as for St Dominic and the mendicant orders they both established, the world held little danger; Christianized at last, it had itself become their monastery. As St Francis expressed the new mood in his 'Canticle of the Sun':

O most high, almighty, good Lord God, to thee belong praise, glory, honour, and all blessing!

Praised be my Lord God with all his creatures, and specially our brother the sun, who brings us the day and who brings us the light; fair is he and shines with a very great splendor: O Lord, he signifies to us thee!

Praised be my Lord for our sister the moon, and for the stars, the which he has set clear and lovely in heaven.

Praised be my Lord, for our brother the wind, and for air and cloud, calms and all weather by which thou upholdest life in all creatures.

Praised be my Lord for our sister water, who is very serviceable unto us and humble and precious and clean.

Praised be my Lord for our mother earth, the which doth sustain us and keep us, and bringeth forth divers fruits and flowers of many colors, and grass.

Praised be my Lord for all those who pardon one another for his love's sake, and who endure weakness and tribulation; blessed are they who peaceably shall endure, for thou, O most Highest, shall give them a crown.

Praised be my Lord for our sister, the death of the body, from which no man escapeth. Woe to him who dieth in mortal sin! Blessed are they who are found walking by thy most holy will, for the second death shall have no power to do them harm.

Praise ye and bless the Lord, and give thanks unto him and serve him with great humility.[69]

By glorifying the natural world as an evidence of God's immutable goodness, St Francis also sanctified everyday toil. In the Franciscan view of things, man was himself a creature of nature, and since to work at one's trade was to preserve one's existence, even the most commonplace of activities became a form of praise for the Creator to whom all mankind owed its being. As a result, natural human desires were suffused with supernatural meaning, and acceptance of life in this world no longer seemed to war with the hope of salvation.

In the course of the century, this theme came to dominate much of popular literature, notably those tales that celebrated the love of the Virgin. Of these, none is more famous than *Our Lady's Tumbler*, the story of a wandering acrobat who, increasingly wearied by the cares of the world, decides to enter the monastery of Clairvaux. Yet life with the Cistercians proves unexpectedly hard:

Of a truth, he had lived only to tumble, to turn somersaults, to spring, and to dance. To leap and to jump, this he knew, but naught else, and truly no other learning had he, neither the 'Paternoster', nor the 'Canticles', nor the 'Credo', nor the 'Ave Maria', nor aught that could make for his salvation. He was sore affrighted in their midst, for he knew not what to say, or what to do of all that fell to be done there.

For months his agonies continue, but eventually he discovers a solution: Avoiding the other monks, forever busy with their offices, he flees to the crypt where, in front of the Virgin's image, he devoutly performs the few tricks he knows. Happily tumbling and somersaulting to the point of exhaustion, he finds his exertions eventually rewarded, for when the abbot learns of these 'blasphemous' activities, he rushes to the crypt, only to see the Virgin herself in descent from the vaulting:

Her vesture was all wrought with gold and precious stones, and with her were the angels and the archangels from the heavens above, who came around the tumbler, and solaced and sustained him. . . . And the sweet and noble Queen took a white cloth, and with it she very gently . . . fanned his neck and body and face to cool him, and greatly did she concern herself to aid him, and give herself up to the care of him; but of this the good man took no heed, for he neither perceived, nor did he know, that he was in such fair company.

Overcome with emotion, the abbot can only marvel at the mercy of God, while the narrator hastens to stress the point of the story:

Think you now that God would have prized his service if that he had not loved Him? By no means, however much he tumbled. But He prized it because of his love. . . . Cheerfully did he tumble, and cheerfully did he serve, for the which he merited great honour, and none was there to compare unto him. . . . Now let us pray God, without ceasing, that He may grant unto us so worthily to serve Him, that we may be deserving of His love. The story of the Tumbler is set forth.[70]

In such literature the basic principles of the new integration were most universally expressed, and they were to appear again in more philosophical form as a major underpinning of Thomistic theology. St Thomas Aquinas was a Dominican, and like most mendicants of the day, he rejected the sharp dividing line that had traditionally separated nature from supernature, reason from revelation. 'Grace', he affirmed, 'does not deny nature, but perfects it', and in his *Summa Theologica* he went on to demonstrate how the whole of God's Being and purpose, as revealed in the Bible, could be understood as the logical culmination of that knowledge which man already possessed on the basis of his reason alone. Most earlier Christians had taken a contrary position. St Paul had proclaimed that Christ had made foolish the wisdom of this world, while Augustine had argued that man without grace lived in a state of near total depravity. Such views had received general acceptance, and that they had helps to explain why medieval thinkers should so often have shown a fine disregard, at least outwardly, for the accomplishments of classical philosophy: since man lived under the burden of sin, the data gained from his senses were not to be trusted, let alone his speculations about what they might mean.

With the thirteenth century, however, these assumptions began to change, largely as a consequence of St Thomas' brilliant defence of Aristotle. To the twelfth century, Aristotelian thought had appeared heretical, for it relied on sense experience for knowledge and, more troubling still, it seemed to imply both that the world had existed uncreated from eternity and that the Prime Mover, God, could never have cognizance of (and hence will the salvation of) individual souls. Unsurprisingly, much of Aristotle had been banned soon after his metaphysical works became known, and though some theologians, notably Albertus Magnus, had attempted to rehabilitate his views, it was only with Aquinas that acceptance became complete. No obstacle was too great for his intellect: subtly analyzing here, deftly probing there, Thomas created an interpretation of the Aristotelian corpus in which the position of this pagan philosopher seemed fully compatible with the fundamental beliefs of Christian revelation.

Although Aquinas' conclusions understandably scandalized the theologically conservative, they followed inexorably from his basic premise, that if God had made man and the universe, then human reason had necessarily to reflect aspects of the Divine; if so, it then further followed that man's thought processes, when properly applied, were adequate for comprehension of some of those laws by which the Creator of the world had chosen to govern it. For Thomas, any other conclusion would have denied God's fashioning of man in His own image, a truth for which the Bible stood witness; indeed, to him the validity of the whole argument was doubtless self-evident, for had he not already demonstrated the harmony between human knowledge and religious dogma? That by itself was surely a proof that man at least partially shared in the rational attributes of his Maker. Thanks to such premises, St Thomas could effortlessly incorporate the whole of human experience into an all-embracing vision of God's plan for salvation. Everything had its place, and in his writings no topic seemed too trivial for discussion, whether it was a question of just prices in business, the movement of angels, or of the possible separation of the soul from the body at the moment of orgasm. His was a synthesis that mingled the practical with the bizarre, but always in a framework that rigorously subordinated each part to the whole.

Though unquestionably the greatest thinker of his age, Aquinas was scarcely unique in the techniques he employed. Thanks to the schools, many of them now become universities, standard methods of analysis had arisen, most of them based, like his, on the logical reconciliation of presumed opposites. With scrupulous attention to the smallest details, scholars dissected contrary statements, showing how some were wrong and others misunderstood: usually, the result of such labours was a coherent and unified view of earth and cosmos in which harmony was seen as the necessary consequence of monotheistic creation. Because the age was universal in outlook, its favourite forms of publication were the *summa* and the encyclopaedia. Men sought eagerly after all knowledge, both human and divine, and every scrap of evidence had to be incorporated into their conclusions. Thanks to this tendency, thirteenth-century books occasionally resembled nothing so much as hodgepodges of ill-digested and incredible information, but they should nevertheless be judged for what they were: idealistic and frequently naïve attempts to encompass the whole of man's experience within the confines of a limited number of pages.

Yet, while thirteenth-century intellectual assumptions arose in the universities, the resulting synthesis owed much to the vitality of the towns.

Universities themselves were a city phenomenon, made possible by mercantile wealth, and the mendicants, first popularizers of the new view of the world, were to find their greatest opportunities within an urban setting, either as evangelists to those whom the parish clergy had missed or as professors lecturing to students on the meaning and nature of God. But towns were more than a catalyst for religious and intellectual ferment; through their commerce they reached out to all parts of the known earth, thereby widening men's understanding and deepening their appreciation for the universality of the human condition. The medieval merchant was not, by and large, an impressively reflective person, but to him the atmosphere of the period owed a good deal of its unique flavour.

By 1200, towns and their commerce were well established and thriving; the great battles over charters and liberties had abated, and throughout most of Western Europe the bourgeoisie enjoyed increasing royal protection. Towns no longer had to fear for their very existence – the kings saw to that – and though they continued to have problems, they resulted largely from the high price at which royal benevolence had to be bought. In 1260, for example, the city fathers of Noyon gave the following picture of their finances to St Louis' fiscal agents:

When the king went abroad [on his first Crusade in 1248] we gave him fifteen hundred pounds and while he was away the queen informed us that he was in need of money and we gave him five hundred pounds. And when the king returned we lent him six hundred pounds. We have only received one hundred pounds back and we gave him the rest. And when the king made his peace with the King of England [in 1259] we gave him twelve hundred. And each year we owe the king two hundred pounds Tournois for the commune we hold of him and every year our presents to visitors cost us at least a hundred pounds or more. And when the Count of Anjou [St Louis' brother] was in Hainault, we were told that he needed wine and we sent him ten casks which cost us a hundred pounds in all. Afterwards he let us know that he needed sergeants to maintain his honour and we sent him five hundred which cost us at least five hundred pounds or more. . . . And when the count was at Saint Quentin, he sent for the Commune of Noyon and it went there to preserve his person and that cost us at least six hundred pounds . . . and all this the town of Noyon did for the count in honour of the king. After the departure of the army we received information that the count needed money and would become infamous if we did not help him; we lent him twelve hundred pounds and released him of three hundred to have his acknowledgment of the nine hundred pounds.[71]

Needless to say, such dolorous tales of financial woe should be taken with more than a grain of salt, for, burdensome though royal demands undoubtedly were, little suggests that they exceeded the ability of most towns to pay. Indeed, because monarchs sometimes displayed surprising ingenuity when in pursuit of new revenue, mayors and aldermen soon became equally adept in evading the worst of their masters' exactions. Ever resourceful, they joined pleas of poverty to a host of other manœuvres, but seldom more outrageously than at Arras in 1295: pressed for an aid by the king's cousin, Robert of Artois, the town government met the situation by turning over a perfectly worthless promissory note for five thousand pounds that it had earlier received at a time of royal forced loans.

As the example implies, the thirteenth-century bourgeoisie had learned to handle its political and financial affairs with remarkable ease. No longer a new class, more notable for energy than skill, it had successfully acquired the sophistication and experience to transact its business both at home and abroad. European merchants now roamed the known world. From the East came spices and silks, imported by the Italians and transhipped to the North; from the Baltic came forest products, wheat and dried fish, this last of particular importance to a society in which religious fasts were frequent and long-lasting. Flanders supplied cloth: England and Spain, wool: and France, wine. No region or country was without its speciality, and few failed to find their place in international trade.

Eight times a year, great fairs were held in Champagne, where goods from the North were exchanged for those from the South, thereby saving the merchants of each region the trouble and expense of travelling to far-distant markets. Moreover, since the transport of specie was itself a nuisance, bankers also made a first appearance, developing letters of credit and bills of exchange through which a confusing welter of commercial transactions could be more expeditiously handled. Fairs seemed constantly filled with pandemonium and chaos, and they seldom closed without acrimonious dissension, but out of them emerged both the techniques of nascent capitalism and much of the wealth on which the success of the towns was ultimately based.

Further, by the second half of the century, commercial horizons began to extend beyond the confines of Europe and the Mediterranean basin even to the limitless expanses of China. Before his death in 1227, Genghis Khan had conquered most of the East and had succeeded in establishing a unified Mongol empire stretching from the Black Sea to the Pacific. Though pagan in belief, the Mongols had early expressed an interest in Christianity, and fired by the hope of converting them, popes in the 1240s had dispatched hardy Franciscan missionaries to preach to the Great Khan himself. These efforts proved unavailing, but they did serve to awaken Europe to the possibilities of commercial expansion, and it was with this purpose in mind that Marco Polo arrived as a youth of twenty-one at the court of Kublai Khan in 1275. Narrating his adventures some twenty years later, Marco still found himself filled with the wonders of what he had observed, wonders that he felt moved to relate 'for the benefit of those who could not see them with their own eyes':

Ye Emperors, Kings, Dukes, Marquises, Earls, and Knights, and all other people desirous of knowing the diversities of the races of mankind, as well as the diversities of kingdoms, provinces, and regions of all parts of the East, read through this book, and ye will find in it the greatest and most marvellous characteristics of the peoples especially of Armenia, Persia, India, and Tartary, as they are severally related in the present work by Marco Polo, a wise and learned citizen of Venice, who states distinctly what things he saw and what things he heard from others. For this book will be a truthful one.

It must be known, then, that from the creation of Adam to the present day, no man, whether Pagan, or Saracen, or Christian, or other, of whatever progeny or generation he may have been, ever saw or inquired into so many and such great things as Marco Polo. . . .[72]

Despite the obvious conceit – or possibly because of it – this passage conveys something of the qualities that made the bourgeoisie such an important element in the gradual cohesion that took place in the thirteenth century. Marco himself was unique, and he had seen parts of the world undreamt of by most Europeans; yet, for all the 'diversities of the races of mankind', his viewpoint is essentially unified by his Christian assumption that every people, 'whether Pagan, or Saracen, or Christian, or other', live in a universe created by God, the history of which stretches from 'Adam to the present day'. As in scholastic thought, seeming contraries are reconciled even in the realm of practical experience through an appeal, largely unconscious, to the ultimate unity of the Creator.

Reconciliation was everywhere a theme in urban life, whether in the pie-powder courts which based their decisions on a universal law merchant, or in the municipal governments which attempted to regulate and harmonize the competing interests of gilds and citizens alike. But nowhere did it achieve more noble or lasting expression than in the construction of those Gothic cathedrals which came to dominate every prosperous town and whose very magnificence stands as a perpetual monument both to the wealth and the faith of their builders.

Gothic architecture made its initial appearance in the Ile de France toward the middle of the twelfth century, and from the beginning it seems consciously to have been designed as an architectural style in which the synthesis of contrary elements could be vividly and concretely displayed. Abbot Suger, whose restoration of St Denis is considered a prime source of the style, held almost as a first principle the proposition that:

The admirable power of one unique and supreme reason equalizes by proper composition the disparity between things human and Divine; and what seems mutually to conflict by inferiority of origin and contrariety of nature is conjoined by the single, delightful concordance of one superior, well-tempered harmony.[73]

Completely dominated by these synthesizing views, Suger then happily reported that in carrying out the restoration of his abbey-church, his 'first thought was for the concordance and harmony of the ancient and the new work'.[74]

As Gothic style expanded outward from the Ile de France, it became ever more elaborate, but wherever it appeared, it retained as a basic presupposition the reconciliation and balancing of opposite forces. In a purely structural sense, this integration expressed itself in a variety of still familiar features: the natural horizontal progression of the nave met and blended with the verticality of piers, columns and shafts; flying buttresses countered and supported the outward thrust of high-soaring vaults; rose windows in the transepts and west façade appeared harmoniously to interact with pointed arches to which they bore no coherent relationship. The whole of each church was presented with logic and with an extreme functional clarity that sought forever to demonstrate the builders' faith in the unity that underlay all clashing diversity.

Moreover, if Suger's hope had been to bridge 'the disparity between things human and Divine', that aspiration soon became universal in Gothic. Architects strove to rework massiveness into edifices of seeming delicacy and grace; through the use of a profusion of windows, glaziers attempted to melt and dissolve the solidity of stone under the soft play of warm colours streaming in from above. Gothic cathedrals were designed to give the impression of limitless space, and the consequence, wholly intended, was the creation of places of worship where finite, transitory human beings could feel themselves symbolically confronted with the infinite and eternal mystery of God.

Gothic sculptural programmes displayed a similar intent. At Chartres, for example, the right tympanum of the west façade is devoted to the Incarnation of Christ, but its full meaning would certainly elude the casual observer. Christ is there three times depicted: first as the Babe placed on an altar-like manger: then as the Child presented in the Temple; and finally, in the top panel, as a Child seated on His mother's lap, surrounded by angels. As a border, the Seven Liberal Arts are portrayed, all accompanied by their most famous exponents, most of them pagan. This tympanum is an unusually fine, though not untypical, example of the skill with which Gothic sculptors sought to combine different levels of meaning. The progression from Christ as Babe to Christ as worshipped by angels underscores the dogmatic reality that He was both God and Man, joined in hypostatic union: further, since He is closely identified with the Virgin in all three panels, Mary's unique relationship to the Divine is stressed, especially the fact that she was truly the mother of God, and not just of His humanity. Such a theme was surely appropriate for a cathedral dedicated in her name.

Moreover, that the Babe lies on an altar-like manger has several implications. The symbolism recalls not only the sacrifice of the crucifixion, but also, in so far as the swaddling clothes are fashioned to resemble a loaf of bread, the sacrifice of the mass. Indeed, because Christ Himself is portrayed as bread, the newly proclaimed doctrine of transubstantiation received vivid and concrete support.

Lastly, the scene in the Temple. It was there, of course, that Christ so astounded the Rabbis with His knowledge, and in the central panel He is shown discoursing with them, an action that emphasizes that in His Person is to be found the embodiment of Divine Wisdom. As a result, the meaning of the surrounding border at last becomes clear: the Seven Liberal Arts, the essence of human understanding, are both compatible with Divine Wisdom and useful as tools in the elucidation of God's word. Again, this was surely an appropriate theme for Chartres, the fame of whose cathedral school had spread throughout the countries of Europe.

In sum, Gothic cathedrals and their art everywhere displayed that 'single, delightful concordance of one superior, well-tempered harmony' of which Suger had longingly written, and while much of the credit for the success of this synthesis must be given to the clerics and artisans who planned and created it, not a little is also owing to the society which supported them in their efforts. For Gothic architecture would never have achieved such widespread dominance without the enthusiastic gifts of the faithful, and to examine the actual construction of a church is to appreciate the extent to which people of all conditions became an integral part of the process.

The cathedral of St Julian at Le Mans is of ancient foundation, though its actual origins are shrouded in pious obscurity. Some allege that Julian himself had been sent by Pope Clement I, third successor to Peter, to convert the tribes of Anjou and Maine, while others maintain, probably with greater accuracy, that he could have arrived only centuries later. In any event, all agree that this missionary established the church of Le Mans. Under Julian, the cathedral seems to have consisted of nothing more than the Roman governor's palace, converted to ecclesiastical use, but it was subsequently to be many times rebuilt and enlarged. The sixth-century version lasted three hundred years, until the Vikings sacked and burned it around 865 and again, more disastrously, in 893. The structure that followed, though heavily modified in the eleventh century, then endured into the 1100s, at which point a new nave was constructed in Romanesque. It is this nave, completed in 1154 under the episcopacy of William of Passavant, which stands to the present day.

By the opening of the thirteenth century, however, the canons found the choir of St Julian's no longer suitable, and in 1217 they decided to rebuild it, this time, as it turned out, in high Gothic. The project's first donor was the king, Philip Augustus, for his permission had to be gained in order to tear down the old Roman walls of the town, which threatened to impede the progress of the contemplated expansion. Royal assent came in November, and as a token of gratitude the chapter of Le Mans was to celebrate Philip's anniversary with memorial masses down to the time of the French Revolution.

Construction proved painfully slow – the choir was consecrated only in

1254 and probably not completed much before 1275 – but the burdens of these years were considerably lessened by the flood of pious donations which testified to the high esteem in which such holy work was universally held. As was to be expected, St Louis showed greater generosity than his grandfather, Philip Augustus, for he found it possible to give one hundred pounds plus the royal estates at Courgenard and Cormes. His brothers, Alphonse of Poitiers and Charles of Anjou, contributed landed revenues and precious relics respectively, while his minor son, Peter of Alençon, joined father and uncles in similar, though smaller gifts. Followers of the king and his family also added their mite to the swelling totals, and at Alphonse's death it was discovered that he had bequeathed a further thirty pounds. From all over France clerics provided considerable sums of money, for in this age of cathedral building no one was more aware than Churchmen of the pressing need for cash under which the chapter of St Julian's constantly laboured. In the list of donors appear the names of such prelates as the archbishop of Rouen and the bishops of Dol and Avranches, and it seems likely from the records that their deans and canons were encouraged to give with them. More touching, perhaps, were the modest contributions of Rogesius and Stephen, humble monks of St Denis; in their small way, they continued the traditions of Suger.

Within the county of Maine, donations become too numerous to mention; whether noble or cleric, peasant or bourgeois, every man did what he could. At Le Mans itself, even the architects and glaziers of the choir gave toward the furtherance of their own work, and among the commercial gilds of the town a fierce competition developed as vintners, drapers, furriers, bakers, moneyers and innkeepers all strove to surpass each other in generosity. The wine gild, for example, initially planned to endow the altar with candles, only to find that the bakers had already seen to this need. Nothing daunted, the vintners quickly agreed on another gift, one whose marked superiority they were careful to emphasize in the charter of donation: 'Others have given transitory lights,' it said, 'but we shall give a window that will light the church for eternity.' And possibly the charter was right, for though the bakers have long since ended their purchase of candles, this window, high in the clerestory, continues to show the wine gild at work as it has for the past seven centuries.

The undeniable charm of this story does much to explain why the Middle Ages have had an enduring appeal for writers like Henry Adams, men hostile to the values of their own day and anxious to retire to some calm centre of peace in the realm of the imagination. To light a church for eternity is hardly a modern ambition, but few people can even now fail to respond to the gift of the wine gild or, by extension, to the society in which such events could take place.

At the same time, however, the writer who falls in love with his own pre-

The Sumptuous Life of the Nobility

For high-ranking nobles like John, Duke of Berry, banquets were an occasion for ostentatious display.

Overleaf: hunts gave an excuse for many and varied diversions – a detail from a fifteenth-century tapestry showing a deer hunt.

Less elevated pleasures were provided by boat tournaments (*top*), parlour games (*centre*), and hockey. From the *Heures de la duchesse de Bourgogne*.

conceptions about an ideal Middle Ages runs the obvious risk of obscuring the extent to which the thirteenth-century synthesis was the creation of ordinary men, all of them subject to the normal temptations of flesh. For example, the wine gild of Le Mans may have showed undeniable religious commitment in the dedication of its window, but its attempt to light St Julian's for eternity seems equally to have been motivated by a very human desire to denigrate the bakers and their contribution. Similarly, if the Church has canonized St Thomas Aquinas and proclaimed him 'the Angelic Doctor', contemporary opponents of this theology rather more plainly dubbed him 'the Dumb Ox' and happily made fun of his immense bulk and ponderous movements. In short, sainthood was hardly a quality that was universally shared.

Moreover, no age has ever successfully legislated the morality of its people, and in this the thirteenth century proved no exception. St Louis attempted to end prostitution in France, but his efforts came to naught when the bourgeois of Paris protested that their wives and daughters could no longer safely appear on the public streets. Everywhere bastards were common, and rape hardly less so; in England, harsh penalties confronted the noble 'who covers a maid without her thanks', but legal severity did nothing to end the practice.

To some extent, the thirteenth-century synthesis became possible only because those in authority were generally willing to bend to human frailty and to permit a certain amount of license within the system. Thus, unlike Louis IX, the bishop of Lincoln was typical of his age in granting ecclesiastical sanction for the brothels of London; regulation was preferred to prohibition, and the understanding displayed by the Church in such matters usually received ample reward in the form of generous gifts from those women who found it difficult to abandon their ancient profession. Even in this most religious of centuries, bishops judged it expedient to allow the parody of religion itself, and in the various Feasts of Fools that flourished all over Europe, one can discern the joy of people momentarily liberated from the pressures of external constraint. In northern France, the lesser clergy annually celebrated the Feast of the Ass, a mock mass honouring the humble beast which had so patiently borne Mary to Bethlehem: in this service, the stench of burning shoes replaced the odour of incense, and at the elevation of the host, churches rang not to the sound of bells, but of braying. During a similar ceremony in England, a prostitute would be installed on the episcopal throne and a fool selected as king by the populace; the rest of the day would then be spent in revelry and debauches, interrupted only by shows of extreme deference to the 'king' and his court.

Further, though universities were the wellspring of scholastic theology, the exuberance of their students has seldom been equalled. Paris received its first charter following a violent riot in 1200, and Cambridge appears to have been founded in 1209 by scholars fleeing the all-too-frequent town-gown disputes at Oxford. Regulations constantly forbade the carrying of arms, and surviving copybook letters suggest that the ways of students have undergone remarkably little change in the past seven centuries. In one, for example, a father angrily reproves his son in wholly familiar terms:

I have recently discovered that you live dissolutely and slothfully, preferring license to restraint and play to work and strumming a guitar while the others are at their studies, whence it happens that you have read but one volume of law while your more industrious companions have read several. Wherefore I have decided to exhort you herewith to repent utterly of your dissolute and careless ways, that you may no longer be called a waster and your shame may be turned into good repute.

Yet, while fathers even then could take sons to task for what one referred to as 'indulging in sport and in certain other dishonorable practices which I do not now care to explain by letter', correspondence from students often seems just as familiar:

B. to his venerable master A., greeting. This is to inform you that I am studying at Oxford with the greatest diligence, but the matter of money stands greatly in the way of my promotion, as it is now two months since I spent the last of what you sent me. The city is expensive and makes many demands; I have to rent lodgings, buy necessaries, and provide for many other things which I cannot now specify. Wherefore I respectfully beg your paternity that by the promptings of divine pity you may assist me, so that I may be able to complete what I have well begun. For you must know that without Ceres and Bacchus Apollo grows cold.[75]

Needless to say, fools' masses, prostitutes and student frivolity in no way deny the existence of a new integration, but they do serve to place it in better perspective. While developing an essential unity of outlook, society had also made provision for deviation from the norm, and it may very well be that the period's successes depended in large part on the ready availability of acceptable means for the expression of feelings and attitudes not normally compatible with men's fundamentally religious assumptions. Because ribaldry, irreverence and carnal pleasures were permitted a recognized forum, they posed no threat to the continuing validity of the social order; on the contrary, the very ease with which they could be practised, often under clerical sponsorship, did much to foster an increasingly confident belief that men had at last discovered how to reconcile their ways with God's.

Nevertheless, this relative tolerance had its limits. Society was, after all, profoundly Christian in origins and outlook, and while it could accept the sins of the flesh with reasonable composure, it proved totally incapable of making a place for people whose religious values differed from its own. Christianity had so permeated all aspects of life that those not sharing in the faith found themselves excluded from even the most commonplace of activities. Membership in the gilds was denied to them, for gilds were religious organizations, established to honour the saints; similarly, every normal legal procedure lay beyond their grasp, for law depended on oaths, the sanctity of which was ensured by the Gospels and relics on which they were sworn: since such objects had little meaning for non-believers, their word was not to be trusted. Moreover, in so far as the harmony of the thirteenth century was ultimately based on the conviction that discord was impossible in a world which the one Christian God had made, difficulties inevitably arose as soon as Jews and heretics entered the picture. They accepted none of society's religious presuppositions, and in practice their obstinacy proved highly resistant to the most subtle forms of persuasion. As a result, they seemed a canker on the body politic, people whose sins had utterly blinded them to the ways of divine truth. Little wonder, then, that like all cankers they were feared as a positive danger, one that had to be cauterized and eliminated before the contagion could spread, thereby infecting even the faithful with views that would forever deny them the possibility of salvation.

Here the limitations and flaws of the thirteenth-century synthesis are most apparent, for if the age of St Francis was a time of Gothic and *summae*, it also saw pogroms and the creation of the Inquisition. Dominicans became the chief pursuers of heresy, and for their efforts they were known as *Domini canes*, the 'hounds of the Lord'. Few would have considered it a term of opprobrium. In much the same way, St Thomas Aquinas, far from being repelled by the horrors of inquisitorial proceedings, could actually defend them under the doctrine of charity. And though St Louis was normally the mildest of men, his biographer Joinville recorded a different attitude with regard to the Jews:

The King told me also that there was once a great debate at the monastery of Cluny between clerks and Jews. There was a knight present who had been charitably fed at the monastery by the Abbot for the love of God. He asked the Abbot to allow him to be the first to speak, and rather unwillingly his request was granted. He stood up, then, and, leaning on his crutch, he asked them to bring the most learned of the clerks and the greatest master of the Jews. This they did; and he asked but one question, which he put so: 'Master', said the knight, 'I want to know whether you believe that the Virgin Mary, who bore God in her womb and in her arms, gave birth a virgin, and whether she is indeed the Mother of God.'

The Jew answered that he believed no such thing. Then the knight told him that it was indeed the act of a fool to enter her church and her house when he neither believed in her nor loved her. 'And I can assure you,' he added, 'that you shall pay for your folly.' He raised his crutch and struck the Jew on the side of the head, felling him to the ground. The Jews all fled, taking with them their wounded master; and that was the end of the debate.

Then the Abbot came up to the knight and told him that he had been most foolish; the knight answered that the Abbot had been a great deal more foolish to arrange the debate, for before it was finished there would have been a great many good Christians who would have gone away with their faith impaired, having been deceived by the Jews' arguments. 'I agree myself', said the King, 'that no one who is not a very learned clerk should argue with them. A layman, as soon as he hears the Christian faith maligned, should defend it only by the sword, with a good thrust in the belly, as far as the sword will go.'[76]

Perhaps we in the twentieth century should be the last self-righteously to condemn such prejudice and bigotry, but intolerance cannot, for that reason alone, be totally ignored. It was the dark and seamier side of the thirteenth century's achievement, and if cathedrals like Salisbury and Chartres have endured to the present day, monuments to all that was best in medieval Christianity, we must also recognize that so have narrowness and hate, themselves a product of that faith. In defence of medieval man, it can at least be said that he acted sincerely, out of a conviction that his was the way of truth; moreover, simply because he viewed the world under the aspect of eternity, he could see little justification for showing even a temporary mercy to those whom he knew that God in His infinite wisdom would eventually consign to the fires of everlasting damnation. In short, the conscience of medieval man was clear, and repellent though his attitude may now appear, it merely reflected a naïve and credulous honesty to which few modern bigots could hope to aspire.

The exiled Dante was no stranger to intolerance and hate, but human depravity was not the ultimate theme of his work. Rather, his concern was always for salvation, and if *The Divine Comedy* begins with the horrors and dissension of Hell, it concludes with a vision of Paradise and a mystical hymn to the Creator, 'The Love that moves the sun and the other stars'.[77] For Dante, as for all medieval thinkers, man was flawed and sinful, but no amount of bestiality could ever persuade the poet that at the last day unity would not be restored. And in the end, long after the fires of the Inquisition have faded into distant memories, it is to that dream that thoughts most frequently return. Who, then, shall say that the thirteenth century laboured in vain?

8 The Emergence of National Sentiment

History has not been kind to Louis VII of France. Successor to a strong father, he was himself to be succeeded by an even more powerful son, and notable though his own accomplishments were, they pale beside those of Louis VI and Philip Augustus. Moreover, Louis was unlucky in love, never a very auspicious sign, but one which, in his case, appeared doubly unfortunate since it seemed momentarily to threaten the existence of the monarchy itself. It was not, however, entirely Louis' fault.

In 1137, as his father lay mortally ill, word came to the court that Duke William X of Aquitaine had just died, leaving the guardianship of his young daughter and sole heiress to his lord, the king. Louis VI had once been a vigorous man, but of late a growing corpulence had slowed his pace – so much so, in fact, that long before the onset of his final illness he had become unable to mount the saddle from which he had directed his many victories. Yet his mind remained alert to the end, and in William's last wishes he immediately recognized unparalleled opportunity. As guardian, he possessed the right to name the lady's husband, and to that lucky man would fall the enjoyment of her vast inheritance, territories much larger than his own, ones that stretched southwards from the Loire almost to the shores of the Mediterranean. The chance was not to be lost, so it was with understandable pride and exultation that he dispatched his son to meet the bride. It was in this way, then, that the future Louis VII became the husband of Eleanor of Aquitaine.

A greater mismatch would be hard to imagine. Where Eleanor was gay and vivacious, Louis was quiet, pious and austere; while Eleanor patronized poets and sponsored courts of love, Louis listened to sermons and rallied the forces of the Second Crusade. As Eleanor herself was later to put it: 'I thought I was marrying a king, but instead I am the wife of a monk.' Mutual dislike grew apace, ripening gradually into genuine hate, and while marriages of convenience were never exceptional at any time during the Middle Ages, seldom was one more doomed from the beginning than theirs. The real wonder is that it lasted for over ten years, an interval whose length suggests the supreme importance of Eleanor's inheritance in Louis' eyes. The final break came on the expedition to the Holy Land. Why Eleanor should have chosen to accompany the king on such an arduous journey defies comprehension; crusading armies were scarcely a suitable place for women of quality, and certainly not for one as high-spirited as the queen. Undoubtedly, her decision represented little more than a whim of the moment, a passing flight of fancy that hardened into firm resolve when it encountered Louis' opposition, but once taken, it proved her undoing.

Precisely what happened, we shall never be certain. What can be said, however, is that the Second Crusade had to endure unimaginable suffering. Arriving in Constantinople, it aroused nothing but constant suspicion, for the Byzantines greatly feared that this army of Christ might turn against its brethren in the East and attempt to usurp the diadem of the Caesars. Ever subtle, the Greeks decided to lessen this danger by suggesting a route to the Holy Land that was finely calculated to confront the expedition with as many Turks and as little water as possible. The results were as intended: Such Frenchmen as survived the heat, battles and thirst of Anatolia arrived at Antioch in little condition to present much of a danger to anyone.

To every suffering Eleanor was oblivious. She and her coterie continued to seek their pleasures as best they could, disporting themselves at poetry readings and engaging in an endless round of courtly games; all the while they remained completely unmindful of the wretchedness surrounding them. At Antioch, their behaviour became rapidly worse, and rumours began to circulate, most of them remarkably explicit, that the queen's relations with some of her knightly companions were rather less chaste than her high station demanded. Indeed, so exaggerated did these reports later become that she was finally to be accused of adultery with Saladin himself, admittedly a delightful story, though highly unlikely: he was but six at the time. In any event, no matter what actually occurred, after the Crusade's inglorious conclusion Louis hastened to Rome where he conferred long and secretly with the Pope. When Eugenius III proclaimed the marriage's annulment in 1152, the announced grounds were consanguinity.

With Eleanor's departure, Louis VII lost not only a wife, but all hope of control over Southern France. Moreover, the king's difficulties, already great, were soon compounded, for two months later Eleanor became the bride of Henry Plantagenet, count of Anjou and by general agreement prospective heir to the throne of England and the duchy of Normandy. Before another two years were out, Henry had succeeded to these honours and the French monarchy was faced with a threat to its very existence. At first glance, French hopes of resistance seemed slight. Louis had direct control over little more than the Ile de France, and the allegiance of his great vassals – men like the counts of Champagne and Flanders – was tenuous at best. Yet Louis *was* king, and that gave certain advantages. Anointed with holy oil at his coronation, oil that a dove had miraculously borne from Heaven for the crowning of Clovis, he became by virtue of that rite the Chosen One of God, a monarch whose divinely bestowed position was further demonstrated by this thauma-turgic ability to cure scrofula, the king's evil, through a simple laying-on of hands. Sanctification gave Louis no coercive powers over those he attempted to rule, but it did offer a measure of defensive protection, for those who attacked him attacked God, an act of audacity that few were prepared to risk.

As a result, events followed lines that no one could have anticipated. Un-willing directly to challenge the lord of his French possessions, Henry turned first, in 1159, against the count of Toulouse, seeking thereby to acquire lands that would give Aquitaine immediate access to the Mediterranean. In turn, the count appealed to Louis VII, also his lord, and in due course the king arrived at the town of Toulouse, accompanied by an army of no more than seven hundred men, the most he had been able to muster. Nevertheless, small as these forces were, they proved adequate to the task: fearing to start a siege lest any attack be interpreted either as defiance of God or as a pre-cedent for his own vassals to rebel against him, Henry tried desperately to persuade Louis to leave, but when the king remained obdurate, he himself was forced to depart, his hopes of conquest dashed. Though weak, Louis VII had survived his first test.

Over the years, the struggle continued, a series of border wars interspersed with truces, and through thick and thin Louis displayed an amazing capacity to endure. Seldom daunted, he learned to take advantage of every oppor-tunity. When Henry's quarrels with Becket reached fever pitch, the French court was only too eager to offer sanctuary and to intercede with the Pope; similarly, when Henry's sons rose in rebellion, Louis proved equally willing to lend an avuncular ear. Nothing could disturb the equanimity of his dis-position, and though English ambassadors sought diligently to humble his pride with tales of their master's wealth, these efforts were to no avail, for with perfect composure he could serenely if dryly respond: 'We in France have only bread, wine – and happiness.' As Henry was rapidly discovering, and as Louis already well knew, no husband of Eleanor of Aquitaine could dream of making a similar statement.

Yet, in spite of the successes that marked French resistance, one serious problem remained: the lack of an heir to the throne. As Louis' wife, Eleanor had borne only two daughters, and though the king was nearly as quick to remarry as she, the passing years brought nothing but continued barrenness. Feelings of unease began to mount, for Louis was getting no younger, and a son was vitally needed to ensure a succession unmarred by strife. With no heir, civil war seemed inevitable, and if one were to break out, the hopes of the monarchy would in all likelihood be dashed.

It was with relief, therefore, that early in 1165 men learned of the preg-nancy of the queen, Adela of Champagne. And their joy knew no bounds when, on 21 August, she gave birth to a son, Philip Augustus. Bonfires were lit all over Paris, and from every steeple the bells rang out. Writing some fifty years after the event, an Englishman who had then been a student on the Left Bank could still vividly recall the scene. The streets, he said, had been filled with revellers, and when he had attempted to venture forth from his lodgings, he had soon encountered a boisterous group which, recognizing his nationality from the style of his dress, had angrily cried out: 'Englishman, tonight a king is born who will drive you English out of France!'

Although this incident is doubtless apocryphal, the invention of a chronicler trying to lend an air of inevitability to events that were only later to transpire, nevertheless it rather vividly illustrates the first appearance of national consciousness, a phenomenon that was gradually to alter many of Europe's basic assumptions about the nature of political communities. For it was during this period, the height of the Middle Ages, that the inhabitants of now separate countries were beginning to develop an awareness of national identity, and the differing ways in which they did so were to have an incalculable influence not only on political life, but on manners and morals. In earlier centuries, nationalism had been unknown. Different peoples had had differing customs and languages, all of which were jealously guarded, but awareness of a wider community had rested solely on the sense that all men, when properly baptized, were part of that *Populus Christianus* to whom God had revealed the path to salvation. Moreover, with the disintegration of the state, political allegiance had become almost entirely personal, and no one could conceive of bonds of affection or dependence which did not flow more or less directly from the lord-vassal relationship.

In the eleventh century, however, changes occurred. The rise of territorial principalities and the experience of diocesan peace associations created a new context in which men were enabled to see beyond their immediate obligations to a network of mutual responsibilities that bound the people of a region together, regardless of status or feudal position. Much the same process took place in the towns, and the whole development was to culminate in the Crusades, a movement that seemed to unite men on a wider and more practical scale than had ever been previously known.

Nevertheless, if the Crusades were expeditions theoretically launched by the Christian people acting in concert, their reality proved very different. Once gathered together, men from every corner of Europe began to appreciate the linguistic and cultural features that separated them; as leaders quarrelled, so did their troops, and the result was the creation of self-conscious national rivalries in which men from one land would glory in their own accomplishments while scorning the achievements of others. 'Shame on the French,' as the English Geoffrey de Vinsauf was to say, 'for indulging in such excesses!'. Moreover, the Crusades were hardly alone in fostering a deeper sense of national identification. The growth of commerce and travel had similar effects, and in France and England the eventual political victory of centralized monarchies over more local interests ensured that the subjects of each realm would increasingly view themselves within a national context. Here, however, a further debt to the Crusades emerges. No one in the twelfth century appears to have thought of crusading as aggressive or imperialistic; rather, men conceived of it as purely defensive, a 'defence of the Holy Land' in which all Christians were obligated to serve against the forces of darkness. To deny aid was unthinkable, for a threat to the Holy Land was a threat to the mystical body of Christendom itself, and it was well known that those who fell in the cause would achieve martyrdom and salvation.

Such ideas had obvious nationalistic applications, and as early as *The Song of Roland* they found popular expression in the poem's frequently repeated assertion that because Roland and his paladins had died for 'sweet France', a land which God Himself had especially blessed, all were deserving of the martyr's crown. By the end of the thirteenth century, variations on this crusading theme had become so commonly accepted that the sanctified kings of England and France would show no hesitation in endlessly proclaiming that every subject had the duty, almost religious in character, of contributing 'for defence of the realm in times of necessity'. And from the statements of Edward I and Philip the Fair it seems but a small step to Joan of Arc's fervent belief that 'Those who wage war against the holy kingdom of France, wage war against King Jesus'.

Despite similarities, however, national sentiment tended to take varying forms in different countries. England developed a spirit of unity in which every order of society felt itself somehow to be a part, whereas France, much more fragmented internally, found cohesion only in the allegiance of all to the crown. Indeed, during the medieval period at least, some peoples, notably the Germans and Italians, failed to create anything more binding than a vague sense of cultural identification, and this lack was later to prove a source of constant difficulty. The story of French unification begins with Philip Augustus, whose birth had been so ardently celebrated in 1165. And with good cause, for his reign marked a turning point in the wavering fortunes of the Capetian monarchy. Louis VII died in 1180, exhausted from years of struggle, but not until the 1190s, after the Third Crusade, did Philip begin to turn to the problem of his Angevin adversaries. In Richard the Lion-Hearted, however, he faced a military genius of the first water, and try though he did, all his efforts to reconquer the duchy of Normandy met with repeated defeats. Had Richard lived, Philip's place in history might have been less easily assured.

But Richard was not to live, and when John succeeded him in 1199, the king of France at last confronted an opponent more to his liking. Poor John! His rule was one long disaster, and in it, after his little ways had successfully alienated almost everyone else, there came a point at which nearly the only

I

person still willing to speak to him was his eighty-year-old mother, Eleanor of Aquitaine. In this son, apparently, she had finally discovered a man she could love.

As far as Philip was concerned, however, John's difficulties began not with his mother, but his wife. Isabella was heiress to the county of Angoulême, and as such she had in early life attracted the ardent suit of Hugh the Brown, count of neighbouring La Marche, who in marriage saw an opportunity to unite the two family holdings. Moreover, Hugh seems genuinely to have liked the lady, and he was delighted, therefore, to find his court bearing fruit: vows of intended marriage were exchanged, and by 1200 it looked as though Isabella would soon be his. At this point, John intervened. For him, Angoulême was geographically important, a vital link between his posses-sions in the North and South of France, and he feared lest it fall into the hands of one possibly favourable to the cause of Philip Augustus. Since Hugh was momentarily engaged in other affairs, John decided to settle the matter to his own advantage by marrying Isabella himself. The ceremony was performed on 31 August 1200, and though Hugh the Brown was thereby denied a wife, England had gained a new queen.

The rage of the count of La Marche mounted apace, particularly after he learned that John intended to offer no compensation. By Easter of the following year, Hugh and his family were in open rebellion, hotly cam-paigning against Angevin forces, and with equal speed they lodged an appeal at the court of Philip Augustus, strongly protesting the English king's high-handed alienation of Isabella's affections. In this way a train of events was set in motion before the end of which John would richly deserve his sobriquet of 'Lackland'.

In Paris, Hugh's complaints understandably received sympathetic atten-tion. John's treatment of this count, his own vassal, had far exceeded even the crude and uncertain limits of feudal propriety, and Philip Augustus well knew that in condemning the king of England he would have the complete support of his barons. Accepting the appeal, Philip three times cited John to appear to answer charges, and when the latter failed to do so, he was un-ceremoniously deprived of his fiefs and proclaimed a contumacious vassal. As Raoul de Coggeshale, an English chronicler, reported the decision:

The Court of France met and judged that the King of England should be deprived of all the lands which he and his ancestors had held of the King of France up to that time because, for a long time, they had neglected to do the services due for those lands and, on practically no occasion, were they willing to comply with their lord's summons.[78]

Though it was one thing legally to condemn John and quite another actually to dispossess him of his fiefs, the conquest of Northern France proved easier than expected. Philip had behind him both the nobles and cities of the kingdom, and his war chest was unusually full, thanks largely to the irony that, three years before, he had compelled the benighted John to pay a relief of twenty thousand marks for the right to succeed his brother Richard. So it was on English money that the campaign proceeded, and by the end of 1204 the whole of Normandy had fallen to Philip's arms. The other Angevin holdings north of the Loire were not completely subdued before the end of the reign, in 1223, but the next three years were to see completion of the task under Louis VIII, a king who also used the brutalities of the Albigensian Crusade to extend royal control to the vast territories of the counts of Toulouse. In less than a quarter of a century, French monarchs had succeeded in establishing their right to rule throughout their kingdom.

Yet these royal successes were far from creating a sense of national identity. So rapidly had the monarchy expanded its power that its subjects had had little chance to accustom themselves to their new-found unity. Provincial differences abounded, and allegiances often continued to be local and regional. Some areas of the kingdom had last experienced royal rule in the ninth century, and it is nowhere more strikingly illustrated that they did not readily accept it than in the closing chapters of the career of Hugh the Brown, count of La Marche.

Despite flashes of that hot temper which seems to flourish in his native Poitou, Hugh was a thoroughly patient man: he knew what he wanted, and he was perfectly willing to wait until the proper occasion arose. In particular, of course, he wanted Isabella and Angoulême, but no opportunity presented itself before 1216 and the death of John. Then, however, he happily renewed his suit, and in due course the dowager queen of England again consented to become his bride. This time the ceremony was actually performed, and with the nuptial kiss, enjoyment of Isabella and Angoulême were finally his. Unfortunately, however, the marriage proved less successful than might have been wished. Isabella was soon complaining that, though she had once been queen of England, no one accorded her the deference and honour due to that rank. Moreover, her wrath increasingly found a target in the court of France, since 1226 presided over by Blanche of Castile, widow of Louis VIII, regent for the young Louis IX, and a woman whose cold and steely determination was more than a match for her own. Isabella felt certain that all her troubles were Blanche's doing and, consequently, that if only Hugh would rebel against French rule, everything could yet be remedied.

When he resisted her importunings, she retaliated by exiling him from her bed, if not her board. This indignity was perfectly calculated in its effects; the unfortunate Hugh, goaded beyond measure and reason, quickly agreed to enter into correspondence with others equally disenchanted with Blanche and her policies. He rapidly formed a conspiracy, and in 1241 he issued a manifesto justifying his formal revolt:

The French have always hated the Poitevins and they continue their hate; they wish to grind everyone underfoot and to possess everything in their ancient domains and in the conquered countries: they treat us with more contempt than they do the Normans and the Albigensians. A valet of the king does his will in Burgundy, Champagne and in other lands; the barons dare to do nothing without his permission; they are as serfs before him.[79]

Hugh's rebellion proved of short duration, for it was rapidly suppressed by the forces of Blanche and St Louis, the latter finally beginning to come into prominence after years of maternal domination. Yet the failure of this uprising should not be allowed to obscure the extreme provincialism of the sentiments on which its appeal had been based. Normandy, Burgundy, Poitou and Champagne were regarded as little more than conquered countries, and in the whole of Hugh's document there is no sign that any of them were better to be viewed as parts of France. On the contrary, the supposed hatred of the French for the Poitevins seems strongly to suggest that in the count of La Marche's opinion the territorial extent of France ended at the frontiers of the old Ile de France, the land from which St Louis' ancestors had originally sprung.

Provincialism long continued to dominate the French outlook. In 1314–15, for example, nobles throughout the country attempted to gain charters of liberty similar to Magna Carta, but the movement resulted in dismal failure because its supporters found anything beyond regional co-operation impossible. Similarly, when Philip v in 1321 sought to convince his subjects that it would be to the common profit to standardize weights and measures, representatives of the towns refused the proposal, replying tartly that 'their own measures had sufficed rather well for them before'. Indeed, they were to suffice to the end of the eighteenth century, for Philip's was the last effort to be made before the French Revolution. Nevertheless, if provincial differences prevented the formation of any corporate sense of national identification, love and respect both for the monarchy and the person of the king came gradually to provide a symbol of unity that could successfully reconcile the competing elements of French diversity. Such an outcome would greatly have surprised Hugh the Brown, no doubt, but the truth of the matter is that the origins of royal popularity are largely to be found in the reign of the man who had so forcibly put down the count of La Marche's angry rebellion.

For, despite the obvious narrowness of his religious prejudices, St Louis was a ruler who easily captured his people's affections. Chivalrous to a fault, he embodied all that was best in the medieval ideal of kingship: moreover, his reputation for piety soon endowed the monarchy itself with an aura of sanctity such as it had hitherto only imperfectly enjoyed. Above all, however, Louis IX displayed an overwhelming concern for the welfare of his subjects, and he laboured unceasingly to make sure that justice would prevail throughout the kingdom of France.

Few men have been as fortunate in their biographers as Louis. In John, lord of Joinville, he possesses one whose personality was uniquely suited as a foil for his own. Unlike his master, Joinville was no saint, but he had a bluff honesty and directness which enabled him to portray St Louis' virtues, often to the detriment of his own:

Once the King called to me and said to me, 'I hesitate to speak to you of what touches God, for I know the subtlety of your mind; as I wish to ask you a question, I have fetched the two friars you see here.' The question was this: 'Tell me, Seneschal,' he asked, 'which would you prefer – to be a leper, or to have committed a mortal sin?' I could never tell him a lie, and I answered that I would rather commit thirty mortal sins than become a leper. After the friars had gone he called me by myself and made me sit at his feet and said, 'How was it that you gave me that answer yesterday?' When I told him that I was still of the same mind, he said to me, 'That is a wild and foolish way of speaking: you should know that there is no leprosy so ugly as being in mortal sin; for the soul that is in mortal sin is in the likeness of the devil, and that it why no leprosy can be more revolting. . . .'

He asked me whether I washed the feet of the poor on Maundy Thursday. 'God forbid, sir!' I answered. 'No, I will not wash the feet of those brutes!' 'In truth,' he said, 'that was a poor answer; you should not despise what God did as a lesson to us. I pray you, then, first for God's sake and then for my sake, to make it your habit to wash them.'[80]

At times, however, Joinville could give as good as he got. One day in the Holy Land, for example, he was accosted by a group of pilgrims asking to see the king:

I went to the king there where he sat in a pavilion, leaning against the pole of the pavilion; and he sat upon the sand, without a carpet, and without anything else under him. I said to him: 'Sire, there is here outside a great group of people from Great Armenia, going to Jerusalem; and they pray me, sire, to cause the sainted king to be shown to them; but I have no desire as yet to kiss your bones.' He laughed aloud, and told me to go and fetch them; and so I did.[81]

Though such stories convey something of St Louis' warmth and simplicity, they fail to reflect his love for his people, a quality he possessed in abundance. Coming home from his first Crusade, he arrived off Cyprus, only to have his ship strike a rock; the sailors, fearing lest tragedy occur, tried to persuade their ruler to leave:

This was the King's answer: 'Sirs, I can see that if I leave this ship she will be abandoned, and I can also see that there are more than eight hundred persons in her. Every man's life is as dear to him as mine is to me, and no one accordingly will dare to stay in the ship; they will all stay in Cyprus. For that reason I shall not, please God, endanger the many lives that she carries. I shall stay in the ship to save my people.'[82]

Only about St Louis' devotion to justice was Joinville more eloquent:

Often in the summer he went after Mass to the wood of Vincennes and sat down with his back against an oak tree, and made us all sit around him. Everyone who had an affair to settle could come and speak to him without the interference of any usher or other official. The King would speak himself and ask, 'Is there any one here who has a case to settle?' All those who had would then stand up and he would say, 'Quiet, all of you, and your cases shall be dealt with in turn.' Then he would call my Lord Peter of Fontaines and my Lord Geoffrey of Villette and say to one of them, 'Now give me your judgment in this case'.

When those who spoke for him or for the other party said anything which he saw needed correction he corrected it himself. Once in the summer I saw him as he went to the gardens in Paris to give judgment for his people. He wore a tunic of natural wool, a sleeveless surcoat of cotton, and a black satin cloak round his shoulders: he wore no cap, but his hair was well combed, and on his head he wore a hat of white peacocks' feathers. He had carpets spread so that we could sit about him, and all who had business with him would stand around, Then he settled their claims as I have just told you he used to do in the wood of Vincennes.[83]

In St Louis, as in no other monarch, all the elements of the thirteenth-century synthesis were present, and because they were, the regional differences with which France was so badly divided seemed to dissolve into nothingness. Long after the king's death in 1270, men would remember the beneficence of his reign, and if they ever had cause to complain (as they most assuredly did), their protests were seldom to be directed against the institution of monarchy itself. For the monarchy had become a sacred trust, one which alone enshrined the national sentiment, and though those oppressed might often again decide to revolt, until the French Revolution their greatest hope appears always to have been nothing more revolutionary than a 'return to the times of good King St Louis'. And understandably so, for this simple man had tried to protect them. As Matthew Paris once put it, he was 'the king of mortal kings'.[84] Or in the words of Louis' own chaplain, Guibert de Tournai: 'Everybody loves him'.[85] How ironic, therefore, that the absolutism of the seventeenth century should have been built on his achievement. And yet possibly even that is understandable, since without a strong king, France was no nation at all.

Unlike France, Germany in the thirteenth century was to experience disaster. Already badly divided, she found her difficulties further compounded as a result of thirty years' rule by a man who, in his own way, was no less remarkable than St Louis. Contemporaries hastened to call Frederick II 'Stupor Mundi', the wonder of the world, and more recent historians, equally dazzled by his genius, have dubbed him 'the first modern man', but neither title begins to do justice to the full range of his accomplishments or perversities. For everything he attempted appears stamped by a personality that was uniquely his own.

Like Louis IX, Frederick was a crusader, but with a difference. In 1215 he promised Innocent III to undertake a voyage to the Holy Land; by 1227, however, the expedition was still unlaunched, and when, under papal prodding, it finally departed, disease soon forced its return to port. Furious, the then pope, Gregory IX, summarily excommunicated the emperor for the delay. Stirred again into action, the latter re-embarked in 1228, only to find himself the target of a second excommunication for daring to assume the cross while under the original ban. Finally, after arriving in the Holy Land, Frederick chose not to fight, but to negotiate, and in this he was successful, for the sultan agreed to return Jerusalem to Christian hands. In spite of this triumph – or really because of it – Gregory IX issued his third excommunication, this time for having had amicable dealings with the infidel.

The emperor was further renowned for his scientific experiments. Fascinated by animals, he gathered together a menagerie that had no peer, and his book, *The Art of Hunting with Birds*, remains to this day a standard text for those interested in falconry. Yet many of his investigations had a more sinister cast. Desiring to know whether meals were better to be followed by sleep or activity, he fed two serfs, ordered one to nap while the other hunted, and then disembowelled them both to make his conclusions. In order to prove that Hebrew had been the original language of Adam and Even, he isolated two infants, a boy and a girl, forbidding all to speak to them; unfortunately, however, the experiment was not a success, since before either could utter a word in any tongue, both died. Anxious to learn the properties of the soul, he had a man weighed, suffocated, and weighed again: finding no change, he concluded that two interpretations were possible: either that the soul did not exist or that it was incorporeal. Bizarre activities, perhaps, though thoroughly typical of a person who was reputed to have claimed: 'All the misfortunes of mankind are due to three impostors – Moses, Mohammed, and Christ!'

Whatever else may be said about Frederick II, it seems fair to say that he was not a man well suited for awakening the national sentiments of the German people. On the contrary, he took little interest in their destiny, for his real concerns lay in Italy. Heir both to the Holy Empire and the Norman kingdom of Sicily, he found his ambitions constantly opposed by popes who understandably feared encirclement of Rome by a ruler whose outlook appeared not entirely compatible with their own. Deciding to take his stand in Sicily, Frederick soon made its administrative and legal systems a model of governmental efficiency, and then, backed by Sicilian resources, he attempted to gain control of the North Italian towns. In this strategy, Germany's only importance lay in the troops she could supply, and since Frederick had but little authority there, he was forced to issue a series of appeals to the German princes. To them he promised every imaginable concession, agreeing to abandon remaining imperial claims while leaving to princely discretion the problem of how each territory was to be ruled. In this way, Frederick's rights were bartered for expendable men, and Germany's political fragmentation, which had begun with the Investiture Conflict, now became almost complete. Frederick's death resulted in chaos so great that for over twenty years, until 1273, it proved impossible even to elect a new emperor; as for a sense of nationhood, that had to await the nineteenth century.

In Italy, the failure of imperial policies brought similar ruin. Sicily passed first to the French, then to the Aragonese; the towns of the North turned to fighting each other; and the papacy, though victorious over the most feared of its rivals, was soon to discover that others could more successfully challenge its sway. At the turn of the century, Dante would call for the return of empire, but that was not to be; instead, Italy would become the home of the Renaissance, and in its cultural splendours she would attempt to express her dreams.

Alone among the countries of Europe, England developed feelings of national unity that embraced the aspirations of all her people. One country even before the Norman Conquest, she had long enjoyed the benefits of centralized rule; moreover, her very smallness and the limited size of her population enabled Englishmen more easily to know both each other and the land in which they lived. The result was a kingdom which, though seldom peaceful, could nevertheless take pride in a strong sense of common identity. No one desired the creation of independent, particularistic principalities such as everywhere existed in Germany, France and Italy; rather, all wished to share in the benefits of a truly national government. The real question, the one over which the many constitutional battles of the thirteenth century would be fought, was the extent to which the king could be forced to recognize the right of others to participate in his rule.

Of those seeking to make their voices heard, none had greater claims to the royal ear than the nobility. Barons in any feudal society expected freely to be able to govern their fiefs, but in England, the fact of the Conquest tended to broaden the scope of their expectations, reinforcing a latent belief that no king should ever decide important matters of policy without first consulting his vassals. This was a lesson that Edward I was to learn to his regret when, in the 1270s, he instituted so-called *Quo Warranto* proceedings, the aim of which was to determine by what right men throughout his kingdom were acting in judicial capacities. No court was to be considered valid unless its possessor could show documentary proof that some king had granted him or his ancestors a franchise to hold it.

This policy led to consternation and growing resentment, for few lords could produce such a charter. Many feudal courts went back to the reign of William the Conqueror, and in granting fiefs to his supporters he had seldom bothered to mention the question of judicial rights: In the eleventh century, they were simply assumed. In the thirteenth, however, different conditions prevailed, and most barons were forced to throw themselves on the king's mercy in the hope that Edward himself would see fit to issue the needed

The Art of War

Under the Carolingians, heavy-armed cavalry, newly equipped with stirrups, began to dominate the battlefield.

ETSYRIAM SOBAL· ETCONVERTIT
IOAB· ET PERCVSSIT EDOM INVAL
LE SALINARVM ·XII MILIA·

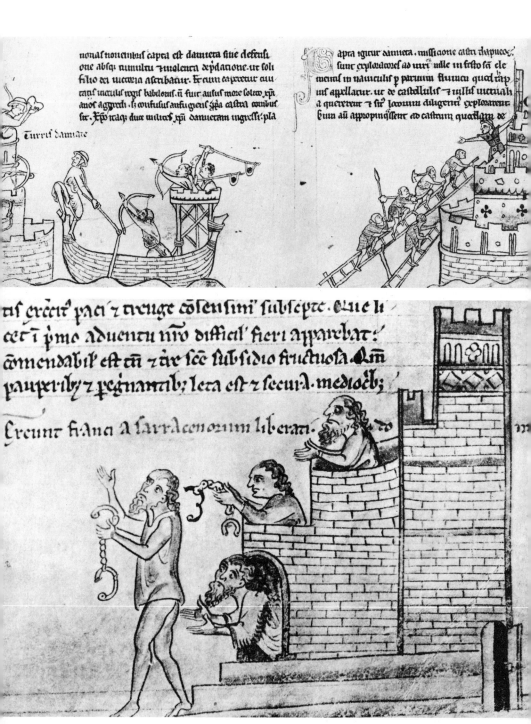

From the eleventh century, castles and fortified towns gave the advantage in sieges to the defence. Here (*top*) foot soldiers assault a castle with axes, arrows and catapults. Few prisoners could look forward to rescue: these crusaders being freed from the Saracens (*immediately above*) were unusually lucky.

Pitched battles were unorganized *mêlées*, characterized more by individual bravery than by discipline and sensible tactics.

At Crécy, the English longbow proved more than a match for French knights and Genoese crossbowmen.

Despite later banking wealth, the Knights Templar were initially poor, as symbolized by this pair (*above*) riding the same horse.

The Battle of San Romano: the vision of mounted combat long continued to hold men's imaginations (Paolo Uccello, painted *c.* 1357).

By the fifteenth century, city walls rarely held out against the increasingly proficient cannons. From Josephus' Siege of Jerusalem.

Some proposals for improving military transport remained artists' dreams (*left*), but better ships helped thirteenth-century crusaders carry the battle to Damietta and other centres of Muslim power (*above*). A successful siege might take many men and months before defenders could be induced to surrender (*bottom left*).

In sea battles, drowning was the usual fate of those swept overboard in full armour.

Encounters between crusaders and Saracens were seldom as friendly as this (*below*).

This statue of St Theodore at Chartres stands as testimony to the chivalrous virtues to which all knights were supposed to aspire.

document. Faced with mounting opposition, he was eventually to do so, but not before he had encountered at least one lord who asked for no mercy. For, according to Hemingburgh's chronicle, when the earl of Warenne was summoned to a royal assize, he appeared, drew a rusty sword, slapped it down on the justices' bench, and proclaimed:

See, my lords, here is my warrant. My ancestors came with William the Bastard and conquered their lands with the sword; with the sword will I defend them against anyone who wishes to usurp them. For the king did not conquer and subdue the land by himself, but our forefathers were with him as partners and helpers.[86]

Even if Hemingburgh's tale had no foundation in fact, its significance would remain the same. For, no matter who first invented this speech, whether chronicler or earl, the real point is that one or both of them felt that the views it expressed were certain to elicit widespread support. After all, the barons' ancestors had indeed accompanied William 'as partners and helpers', and their vague feelings of corporate identity had only been increased by the strong native hostility with which they had been initially greeted. Speaking a different tongue, observing different customs and laws, the Normans had naturally continued to band together until, by the thirteenth century, their descendants formed a class that could begin to demand that the partnership of the Conquest be completed and fulfilled by partnership in the royal government itself. And to achieve this end, the baronage was increasingly prepared to employ that right of rebellion which equally lay at the heart of the earl of Warenne's appeal.

The details of this constitutional struggle are much too familiar to bear repetition; further, though tactics varied with each succeeding crisis, throughout the century the barons showed a remarkable ability to pursue consistent goals, basically no more than a king under law, one whose authority could be hedged in and limited by consent of the governed. Or, to put these aims in language more appropriate to the age, the nobility sought recognition for two principles: first, that 'the law makes the king, not the king the law'; and, secondly, that 'what touches all must be approved by all'. For the barons, these legal maxims were easily grasped and apparently self-evident, but for any monarch, their implications were less acceptable: authority bestowed by the grace of God seemed hardly compatible with authority bestowed by consent of the governed. As St Louis put the royal case in quashing the Provisions of Oxford, Henry III at all times had the right to enjoy 'full power and unrestricted rule within his kingdom and its appurtenances'.[87]

Although these conflicting views were irreconcilable in theory, in practice they proved more amenable to compromise. Thus, if the demands of the Provisions of Oxford struck Henry III as radical in 1258, by the last quarter of the century his son, Edward I, had quietly and calmly accepted many of them. His parliaments may have failed to meet as frequently as the

Provisions had specified, but in membership and jurisdiction alike they significantly exceeded anything of which the baronial reformers had earlier dreamed. So unexceptional had parliamentary discussion of petitions, taxes and statutes become that during the 1290s an otherwise unknown jurist, Fleta, could write that all the great business of the crown had to be conducted by 'the king in his court in his parliament', which was no more than to say, albeit cumbersomely, that most of the barons' objectives had been reached.

Further, this victory belonged not to the nobility alone, for it was shared increasingly by the middle classes. Simon de Montfort had first summoned knights and commoners to his parliaments; Edward I occasionally followed the same practice; and by the fourteenth century few parliamentary gatherings were considered complete unless attended by representatives of the shires and towns. Many battles remained to be fought – and many kings would lose their lives – before constitutional harmony was fully achieved, but as early as the reign of Edward I it seemed abundantly clear that no government could long endure unless it had gained the support not only of the king and his barons, but also of the whole community of the realm. In the much disputed words of Edward II's Statute of York:

And [it is decreed] that henceforth and forever at all times . . . matters which are to be determined with regard to the estate of our lord the king and of his heirs, or with regard to the estate of the kingdom and of the people, shall be considered, granted, and established in parliament by our lord the king and with the consent of the prelates, earls, and barons, and of the community of the kingdom, as has been accustomed in times past.[88]

By 1300, then, the political face of Europe had begun to take on features which would last well into the modern world. Each country had shared in the synthesis of the previous century, but now all were starting down separate paths, the windings of which would profoundly affect the lives of future generations. Italy and Germany lay shattered, prey to the cynical designs of the ambitious. France, though often torn by provincial loyalties, had at last found some measure of unity in the cult of her monarchy, and already the French state was developing symptoms of that absolutism which alone could prevent the onset of total disintegration. As St Louis once explained to Charles of Anjou, whose independence had brought royal disfavour: 'There is only one king in France.' And though England too had only one king, her path had taken a different turning. How Eleanor of Aquitaine would have hated it!

Epilogue
Hard Times and the Chivalric
Afterglow 1300-1450

As the thirteenth century drew to a close, medieval civilization showed signs of ageing. Population ceased to rise; the economy was becoming stagnant; and all over Europe there was a change in mood. Life was losing its gaiety, and during the fourteenth and fifteenth centuries the buoyant optimism that had characterized the long period of expansion gave way to feelings of dread and impending doom from which wild revels and senseless display seemed to provide the only release. Medieval forms continued to prevail, but frequently devoid of content; in the words of Johan Huizinga's now classic work, *The Waning of the Middle Ages*:

> So violent and motley was life, that it bore the mixed smell of blood and of roses. The men of that time always oscillated between the fear of hell and the most naïve joy, between cruelty and tenderness, between harsh asceticism and insane attachment to the delights of this world, between hatred and goodness, always running to extremes.[89]

This new mood reflected not only a crisis in confidence, but a return to hard times; like the world of the millennium, the later Middle Ages were to enjoy few of the comforts to which honest toil is more normally entitled. Economic depression was to grip the age, and, as might have been predicted, the root of the difficulty lay in agriculture.

Population had continued to rise since the eleventh century, and by the end of the thirteenth it had clearly begun to exceed the available food supply. Nowhere was more land to be found; every conceivable acre had already been put to the plough, and often with disastrous results, for in the absence of proper fertilizers and improved technology, many fields proved incapable of yielding an adequate harvest. In France, the last new farming communities were established before 1250, and the next half-century saw the increasing abandonment of tracts whose marginal utility had become distressingly apparent. Given conditions of obvious overpopulation, crop failures posed a constant threat, and the worst fears were to be realized when, from 1315 on, bad harvests followed each other in rapid succession. Prices soared; disease reached epidemic proportions; famine was widespread. Particularly hard hit were the towns. At Ypres, for example, the spring and summer of 1316 brought death to 1,600 of the 18,000 inhabitants; at Bruges, the corresponding figures were 2,500 out of 28,000. Special grave diggers had to be hired, usually paid by the corpse, and everywhere documents referred with laconic brevity to 'the sterility of the times'. Moreover, better harvests did little to improve the situation, for prices then dropped to levels well below those preceding the famine, and peasants, seeing no point in expanding production, began to return to a kind of subsistence farming that would provide for themselves and no one else.

The towns, too, suffered a series of economic reverses, not all of them dependent on the crisis in agriculture. The great textile centres of Flanders encountered increasing competition from other regions of Europe, and their product, a heavy woollen cloth, lost favour to lighter linens and silks, fabrics that were generally manufactured not in towns but as part of a widely dispersed cottage industry. Further, in the 1290s Philip the Fair began a series of Flemish military campaigns that were to continue, almost without let-up, until they were superseded by the even more violent hostilities of the Hundred Years War. Overtaxed, often besieged and plundered, the urban communes had little time for manufacturing and commerce.

Similar conditions came to prevail throughout the continent. New trade routes by-passed the fairs of Champagne, and from 1296 on, their revenues fell precipitously. In the search for money with which to support costly ambitions, monarchs everywhere raised taxes, defaulted on debts, and resorted ever more frequently to debasement of coinage; in turn, financial instability led to hoarding, business failures and a general scarcity of goods. Mounting inflation destroyed purchasing power; labourers fortunate enough to find work received inadequate wages; manorial rents declined; markets simply disappeared. The outbreak of the Hundred Years War only intensified the difficulties of the situation, and in the late 1340s came the greatest disaster of all, the Black Death.

Weakened by half a century of poverty and want, the peoples of Europe were ripe for destruction. How many died, we shall never be certain, though the available statistics are appalling. At Avignon, a town of no more than 100,000 souls, the Plague broke out in January, 1348; seven months later, 62,000 were dead. Seven thousand dwellings were left vacant: 11,000 corpses were interred in the short period from 14 March to 27 April alone. The epidemic reached Givry, in Burgundy, during July. By September, the normal death rate of two per month had risen to over 100 a week, and by the end of the year, 649 had perished. This from a population of some 1,800. Every Franciscan died in Toulouse, and on the Taunton estates of the bishop of Winchester, the death rate, which had been as low as 23 annually in 1346, increased to 707 in 1349. Whatever else may be said, Europe was no longer overpopulated.

But at a psychological cost that can never be measured. Everywhere people became subject to wild and unreasoning terrors. All over Europe the rumour spread that the Jews had poisoned the wells, and the ensuing pogroms were not to be stopped even when Clement VI intervened, placing Jews under his papal protection and threatening excommunication for those who harmed them. Belief in witchcraft reached new heights; frenzied bacchanals and orgies flourished in every land; writers and artists began to introduce a new theme in their works, the Dance of Death. Something of the atmosphere comes through, perhaps, even in the chronicles of Froissart:

This year of our Lord 1349, there came from Germany persons who performed public penance by whipping themselves with scourges having iron hooks, so that their backs and shoulders were torn; they chanted also, in a piteous manner, canticles of the nativity and sufferings of our Saviour, and could not, by their rules, remain in any town more than one night; they travelled in companies of more or less in number, and thus journeyed through the country performing their penance for thirty-three days, being the number of years JESUS CHRIST remained on earth, and then returned to their own homes. This penance was thus performed to entreat the Lord to restrain his anger, and withhold his vengeance; for, at this period, an epidemic malady ravaged the earth, and destroyed a third part of its inhabitants. . . .

About this time, the Jews throughout the world were arrested and burnt, and their fortunes seized by those lords under whose jurisdictions they had lived, except at Avignon, and the territories of the church dependent on the pope. Each poor Jew, when he was able to hide himself, and arrive in that country, esteemed himself safe. It was prophesied that for one hundred years people were to come, with iron scourges, to destroy them: and this would now have been the case, had not the penitents been checked in their mad career. . . .[90]

Catastrophic as the Black Death was, however, it failed to put an end to the Hundred Years War, and in the long run its horrors were more grievous than those of the Plague. For warfare had assumed a new cast: no longer merely the sport of nobles who served their forty days and then returned home to tell of their adventures, it had become a full-time occupation, one in which mercenaries served as the undisciplined instruments of royal policy. Brief summer campaigns gave way to prolonged operations and though battles in winter remained unpopular, their frequency increased. The result was a level of devastation such as never before had been attained.

Since England lacked the resources with which to subdue France, her annual forays across the Channel quickly developed into little more than expeditions in search of booty and plunder. Every year saw wide swathes of countryside laid waste, and when the French tried to resist, as at Crécy and Poitiers, their cavalry was annihilated in a rain of English arrows: as the French learned to their sorrow, knights immobilized under the weight of 130 to 175 pounds of plate armour stood little chance against an army to which the Welsh and Scots had taught not only the use of the longbow, but also the value of fixed positions against which mounted warriors could not hope to prevail. In the end, Charles v and Duguesclin were to turn to guerrilla tactics, daring raids combined with preventive destruction of crops, but while this strategy proved militarily successful, its benefits to the people of France were hardly apparent. For, no matter who burned the fields, their cultivators starved. Moreover, even long truces brought no respite. Mercenaries waged war for profit, and when hostilities ceased or pay gave out, these professionals simply went into business for themselves, raping and looting as the spirit moved them. France became filled with *routiers*, freebooters and *écorcheurs*, these last being the 'flayers' who picked over the leavings that others had scorned. No one seemed able to rid the country of this scourge, and attempts to divert free companies to other lands led only to the introduction of their murderous activities to Italy, Germany and Spain. No scruples restrained the butchery of these men, and so hardened did Europe become to their lack of morality that scarcely a protest was uttered when one group actually held the pope to ransom.

Moving from one defeat to another, the kingdom of France gradually sank into ruin. Though diminished by the Black Death, its population continued to starve, and of all the legends of suffering that arose, few were without basis in fact. Possibly credence should not be given to the story that snails were first eaten by Burgundian monks so reduced by famine that they had no other recourse, but, true or not, even this tale and its happy ending cannot completely obscure the bleak conditions that made such stories credible. Peasants as fortunate as these Burgundian monks were rare indeed, and by the late fourteenth century some regions of France would again be eating acorns and grass.

Political authority fared no better. Signs of impending trouble appeared as early as 1356 when John the Good was captured at Poitiers, for, with the king a prisoner in London, French particularism was given free rein. The members of the Estates-General soon fell to quarrelling with each other and with the Dauphin; Parisian delegates under Étienne Marcel began pressing for radical, almost revolutionary reforms: and by 1358 the peasantry of Northern France had risen in open and violent rebellion. Order returned under Charles v, but tragedy struck in 1392 when his son, Charles vi, became hopelessly, though intermittently, insane. The king's uncles and brothers leapt at the opportunity. Restrained only by occasional moments of royal lucidity, they battled viciously over the division of the pathetically meagre spoils. Rivalries sprouted like dragons' teeth, and in the following struggle no prince could feel safe from assassination. Louis of Orleans was the first to fall, in 1407, and with his death the way was prepared for civil war, Agincourt and Henry v's Anglo-Burgundian alliance. Governmental authority had lost all meaning, and it was to take a miracle to restore it. In 1407, however, Joan of Arc still lay far in the future.

Swept downwards in a maelstrom of their own devising, the French could have found little comfort in recalling how they had earlier brought similar ruin to the papacy and the Church. It had all begun with the differences between Philip the Fair and Boniface VIII, but before the ensuing quarrels had ended, the whole fabric of medieval Christendom had been rent asunder, and Boniface's successors had found it desirable to move to Avignon, where their activities could more easily come under watchful French surveillance.

Hostilities opened in 1296 when the pope forbade the secular taxation of clerics, a decree that struck hard at the kings of England and France, both of whom had long been accustomed to follow this practice. At war with each other and desperate for funds, the two monarchs reacted violently: Edward I proceeded to outlaw the clergy, while Philip the Fair banned the export of gold and silver, a measure that denied the pope a major source of his income. Faced with such opposition – not to mention a growing flood of anticlerical propaganda – Boniface quickly backed down. By the following year, the kings had obtained complete satisfaction, including, in Philip's case, the canonization of his grandfather, St Louis.

The second crisis proved more serious. In 1301 French agents arrested Bernard Saisset, the bishop of Pamiers, charging him with high treason. It was alleged not only that he was guilty of fomenting rebellion in Southern France, but also that he had personally insulted Philip the Fair in rash, intemperate words:

Our king resembles an owl, the fairest of birds, but worthless. He is the handsomest man in the world, but all he knows how to do is stare at people, without speaking. He is neither a man nor a beast; he is a statue.[91]

To Boniface, the possible truth of the charges was irrelevant: what mattered was that, contrary to canon law, a secular ruler was attempting to judge a priest. Moving forcefully, the pope ordered Saisset put at liberty and then summoned the bishops of France to a council in Rome where the affairs of the kingdom would be thoroughly reviewed. Philip, however, remained defiant, so in 1302, at the close of the council, Boniface struck out at royal intransigence in the most famous of all bulls, *Unam Sanctam*:

We are forced by faith to believe in, and hold to, one holy Catholic and apostolic Church. . . . Therefore whosoever resists this power so ordained by God resists the ordinance of God. . . . Whence we declare, say and define that it is altogether necessary for salvation that all human creatures be subject to the Roman pontiff.

The French response was immediate. At hastily summoned assemblies, Boniface was roundly condemned, and Philip's agent, William of Plasian, made it clear that the pope could not escape lightly from the burden of his supposed sins:

I, William of Plasian, knight, say, advance, and affirm that Boniface, who now occupies the holy see, will be found a perfect heretic . . . First, he does not believe in the immortality of the soul; second, he does not believe in life everlasting. . . . He has said that to humble his majesty and the French, he would turn the whole world topsy-turvy. . . . He has had silver statues of himself erected in churches. He has a familiar demon. . . . He is a sodomite. He has had many clerks killed in his presence. . . . He has compelled priests to violate the secrets of the confessional. He observes neither vigils nor fasts. He inveighs against the college of cardinals, the orders of black and white monks, and of the preaching brothers and brothers minor, often repeating that the world was being ruined by them, that they were false hypocrites, and that nothing good would happen to whoever confessed to them. Seeking to destroy the faith, he has conceived an old aversion against the king of France, in hatred of the faith, because in France there is and ever was the splendour of faith, the grand support and example of Christendom. . . .[92]

Nor was Philip to be satisfied with mere polemic. In March 1303 William of Nogaret was secretly despatched to Italy, with orders to return Boniface to Paris for trial; September saw Nogaret and Italian troops storming the papal residence at Anagni; and, though the captured pope was soon freed, a month later he was dead. It was in such ways that the king of France showed himself to be 'the grand support and example of Christendom'.

With Boniface's death, the power of the medieval papacy was effectively at an end, for Rome could hope to preserve its sway only so long as men continued to accept the validity of its authority. And that, clearly, the French were no longer prepared to do. In 1300, for example, when Boniface had protested to Pierre Flote, a royal agent, that the swords of spiritual and temporal authority pertained to the pope alone, he had received the curt reply: 'True, Holy Father, but where your swords are only a theory, ours are a reality.'[93] As Anagni demonstrated, Flote's cynical boast had substance behind it, and the point was again to be made in the following reign: exasperated by the lengthy failure to pick a successor to Clement v, Louis x's brother, Philip of Poitiers, first placed crossbowmen around the church in which the cardinals were meeting; he then bricked up the doors and windows, and finally announced through a small aperture that he would tear off the roof if a new pope were not speedily elected. These tactics bore fruit in the person of John xxii, a Frenchman and close friend of Philip, who found it expedient to give more permanent form to Clement's provisional residency at Avignon. The Babylonian Captivity of the Church had begun.

Like the French monarchy at the end of the century, the Avignonese papacy soon lost all meaningful authority. Few people in Europe were willing to place much confidence in the religious leadership of an institution that seemed so heavily dependent on the wishes of a neighbouring ruler, and the situation became impossibly tangled when, in 1378, the disputed election of Urban vi led to the creation of two lines of popes, one at Rome, the other at Avignon. For almost fifty years the Great Schism was to divide the Church, and the unedifying spectacle of warring curial parties removed the last shred of whatever residual powers the papacy had managed to retain over the faithful.

Moreover, these developments were reinforced by changes in popular religious devotion. The medieval Church had stressed the sacraments as the proper road to salvation, but men in the fourteenth century turned increasingly to a more mystical approach, one in which inward piety and the cultivation of a contemplative spirit replaced the rigid sacramentalism of the clergy. Lay brotherhoods flourished, emphasizing charitable works and the imitation of Christ; gone was the logical formalism of the scholastics, St Thomas Aquinas first among them. For in nominalism, the enemies of the Angelic Doctor had triumphed, and until the sixteenth century and the Council of Trent, the name of Thomism would be seldom invoked.

At the millennium, religion had at least given a measure of consolation to those beset by despair, but part of the horror of the fourteenth century was that religion itself seemed to crumble, thus adding to the woes that political and economic distress had already engendered. Goaded beyond endurance, whole classes of people were moved to revolt, hoping through senseless destruction to make their grievances known. Yet such uprisings did little good, for oppressed and oppressor alike were caught in a web of circumstances beyond the comprehension of either. Rebellion only led to savage reprisals, and something of the resulting tragedy emerges in Froissart's unfriendly account of the French Jacquerie of 1358:

Some of the inhabitants of the country towns assembled together in Beauvaisis without any leader. . . . They said that the nobles of the kingdom of France, knights, and squires were a disgrace to it, and that it would be a very meritorious act to destroy them all; to which proposition everyone assented, as a truth, and added, shame befall him that should be the means of preventing the gentlemen from being wholly destroyed. They then, without further council, collected themselves in a body, and with no other arms than the staves shod with iron, which some had, and others with knives, marched to the house of a knight who lived near, and breaking it open, murdered the knight, his lady, and all the children, both great and small; they then burned the house. . . .

These wicked people, without leader and without arms, plundered and burned all the houses they came to, murdered every gentleman, and violated every lady and damsel they could find. He who committed the most atrocious acts, and such as no human creature would have imagined, was the most applauded, and considered as the greatest man among them. I dare not write the horrible and inconceivable atrocities they committed on the persons of the ladies.

Among other infamous acts, they murdered a knight; and, having fastened him to a spit, roasted him before the eyes of his wife and children, and, after ten or twelve had violated her, they forced her to eat some of her husband's flesh, and then knocked her brains out.

In turn, the nobility soon gained its revenge in the market place of Meaux where men of the count of Foix, the duke of Orleans and the captal of Buch unexpectedly 'posted themselves in front of this peasantry, who were badly armed':

When these bandits perceived such a troop of gentlemen, so well equipped, sally forth to guard the market place, the foremost of them began to fall back. The gentlemen then followed them, using their lances and swords. When they felt the weight of their blows, they, through fear, turned about so fast that they fell one over the other. All manner of armed persons then rushed out of the barriers, drove the peasants before them, striking them down like beasts, and clearing the town of them; for they kept neither regularity nor order, slaying so many that they were tired. They flung them in great heaps into the river. In short, they killed upwards of seven thousand. Not one would have escaped if they had chosen to pursue them further.

On the return of the men at arms, they set fire to the town of Meaux and burned it; and all the peasants they could find were shut up in it, because they had been members of the Jacquerie. Since this discomfiture which happened to them at Meaux, they never collected again in any great bodies; for the young Enguerrand de Coucy had plenty of gentlemen under his orders who destroyed them, wherever they could be met with, without mercy.[94]

Such incidents became a commonplace all over Europe, with peasants and impoverished townsmen savagely rising, only to be repressed with equal savagery by the superior arms of the nobility. And, since the sum total of human misery was thereby increased, the downward spiral continued, an endless series of pathetic attempts to restore order to a world gone mad. To the lower classes, the injustice of their servitude was more and more apparent, and in 1381, during the English Peasants' Revolt, John Ball was to be far from alone in putting his familiar query:

> When Adam dalf and Eve span
> Who was then a gentleman?

For inequality was no longer blindly accepted as part of the human condition, and if Ball's resentment took a form traditional to sermons, the anger of others had a more novel ring. At St Albans, for example, Thomas Walsingham reported that the local leader of the Revolt, William Grindcob, had been quickly imprisoned; nevertheless, when those in authority had released him so that he could calm the passions of his followers, he had unexpectedly decided to encourage their rebellion:

Friends, whom a little liberty has refreshed after so long an oppression, stand fast while you can, and take no thought for what I may suffer; for if in the cause of liberty I must die, I shall think myself happy to end my days as a martyr.[95]

Though Grindcob was hanged for these words, his friends were not easily quelled, and the seeds thus planted were later to bear fruit. But that was to be only long after the end of the Middle Ages.

For the moment, a sombre mood prevailed, and the desperation of the lower orders was further increased by their anguished awareness of the nobility's indifference to their plight. Like the Nero whom Suetonius accused of declaiming while Rome burned, lords and ladies continued to divert themselves with courtly amusements, caring for nothing beyond their own frivolous pleasures. No excuse was too slight for empty festivities, and a royal journey would inevitably become the occasion for endless tournaments, banquets and balls. The expense was incredible, and the lack of compassion even more so. When, for example, Charles VI once made a progress through Southern France designed to investigate and relieve the miseries of its people, the accompanying entertainments proved so costly that the royal treasury was soon emptied; Charles' solution, hardly beneficial to Languedoc, was to levy new salt taxes while further debasing the coinage. The king's enjoyment of life was not to be checked by the mere absence of money.

Grief touched the hearts of the nobility only when its own members suffered, and even then the tears were often short-lived. In 1393, Charles VI held a great wedding feast to honour the marriage of two of his courtiers. The height of the evening came about midnight with the sudden appearance of a group of lords, all disguised as wild beasts; chained together and covered from head to toe with pitch and flax, they proceeded to dance ferociously around the room. The audience was delighted, but tragedy ensued: wishing to know by whom he was being entertained, the duke of Orleans drunkenly seized a torch, approached the revellers, and soon had them in flames. Only Froissart can properly convey the strange mixture of pain, mystification and apathy which greeted the outcome:

Of the four that were on fire, two died on the spot; the other two, the bastard of Foix and the count of Joigny, were carried to their hotels, and died two days afterwards in great agonies. Thus unfortunately did the wedding feast end, although the married couple could in no way be blamed. The duke of Orleans was alone at fault, and he certainly intended no harm when he held the torch so near them. His giddiness caused it; and, when he witnessed how unlucky he had been, he said aloud, 'Listen to me all that can hear me. Let no one be blamed for this unfortunate accident but myself; what has been done was through my fault, but woe is to me that it happened! Had I foreseen the consequences, nothing on earth should have induced me to do it.' The duke then followed the king, and made his excuses, which were accepted. This melancholy event happened on the Tuesday before Candlemas-eve [January 29], in the year of grace 1393: it made a great noise in France and in other countries.[96]

Strikingly, what appears to have bothered Louis of Orleans most about the whole incident was 'how unlucky *he* had been', and in this self-centredness he was thoroughly typical of the age. For him, as for so many of the nobility, the sufferings of others were of little concern; what mattered was simply the preservation of one's own reputation: a good name was to be defended at all costs. Seldom, however, did that imply a life that was reasoned and sensible; rather, nothing was required beyond an ability to perform the proper gesture at the proper time. This the duke knew how to do, and because his apologies were graciously given, they were courteously received. The forms were observed; everyone was satisfied; and no one seems to have worried very much about the fate of the dancers or about the mad circumstances that had led to their demise.

The nobility was equally blind to the realities of the Hundred Years War. In the eyes of its participants, savagery and brutality were transformed into stunning examples of chivalric endeavour, and for such men, filled with romantic visions, Froissart was the perfect apologist. From the opening paragraph of his chronicle, he knew how to set the mood:

That the honourable enterprises, noble adventures, and deeds of arms performed in the wars between England and France may be properly related and held in perpetual remembrance – to the end that brave men taking example from them may be encouraged in their good deeds – I sit down to record a history deserving great praise; but, before I begin, I request of the Saviour of the world, who from nothing created all things, that He will have the goodness to inspire me with sense and sound understanding to persevere in such manner that all those who shall read may derive pleasure and instruction from my work, and that I may fall into their good graces.[97]

And Froissart is successful in his purpose. Under his improving touch, Edward, the Black Prince, no longer appears the vicious, tyrannical despot he actually was; instead, he emerges the chivalrous knight, a man who, though dying, can grandly reply with defiant words to a summons ordering his appearance at the Parlement of Paris: 'We shall willingly attend on the appointed day at Paris, since the king of France sends for us: but it will be with our helmet on our head, and accompanied by sixty thousand men.'[98] Similarly, Froissart can find no stupidity in the decision of John, the blind king of Bohemia, to charge bravely to his death at the battle of Crécy; sightless though he was, he 'made good use of his sword' and 'fought most gallantly'. Moreover, his heroism stood in marked contrast to the cowardice of his son, who, 'when he perceived that things were likely to turn out against the French . . . departed, and I do not know what road he took'.[99]

Such stories reveal more than Froissart's personal code of values. It is a fact, after all, that the king of Bohemia chose to die at Crécy, and while Froissart is the only chronicler to record the Black Prince's disdainful reply, there is little reason to doubt its essential validity: countless similar incidents are known to have occurred, and all of them demonstrate that nobility and rulers alike moved in a world that strongly preferred the chivalrous gesture to sensible policy. After the battle of Poitiers, for example, the captured John the Good was eventually freed upon receipt of the first instalment on his ransom; nevertheless, his liberty proved brief, for when French bankruptcy compelled the cessation of further payments, he voluntarily returned to London where he lived out his days in honoured captivity. To have done otherwise would have been to break his word as a gentleman, and politically advantageous though such a move would have been, it seems never to have entered his head. Much admired by contemporaries, John had nothing to commend him as a ruler; but as a knight, he was the perfect embodiment of chivalrous courtesy. In fourteenth-century eyes, that was enough.

During the fifteenth century, however, new attitudes began to emerge, attitudes that were finally to bring the age of chivalry to a close. The penchant for romantic impulses gave way to greater common sense, and while, by mid-century, the change was far from complete, it was becoming increasingly apparent that cunning, calculation and force were to be the principal virtues on which the successful king would base his rule. It was on such foundations that Henry v attempted to build. Ambitious, determined, and coldly realistic, Henry was no John the Good, and his campaigns little resembled the aimless, disjointed expeditions of Edward III. Unlike his predecessor, Henry set out genuinely to conquer France, and he sought to do so through systematic reduction of strong points followed by permanent occupation. Trainbands of artillery replaced mangonels and catapults in siege operations, while pitched battles saw the full deployment not only of archers, but also of pikemen and halberdiers, new kinds of infantry that proved more than a match for old-fashioned cavalry. Further, Henry's was at last a disciplined army, one in which looting and pillaging were sternly prohibited, for this strong-minded king had begun to realize how unwise was the needless angering of a subject people whose allegiance he had to attract.

In short, Henry took no interest in empty gestures, and though his ambitions still exceeded the limited means at his disposal, his victories stood as proof of what hard-headed realism could at least momentarily achieve. And when, after his death, defeat finally came, it was hardly ascribable to an excess of chivalry, either English or French. Rather, Charles VII and his people had also learned that chivalrous courtesy no longer paid, and in so doing they developed a new outlook which better enabled them to pursue sensible and obtainable goals. Such was the contribution of Joan of Arc.

When, in February of 1429, Joan set off on her mission, France seemed prostrate. At Rouen, Bedford ruled in the name of young Henry VI; at Paris, their ally, the duke of Burgundy, held sway. Even then, English forces lay camped beneath the walls of Orleans, pressing their siege, while the Dauphin, helpless and neglected, was to be found only at Chinon, a small town on the Loire, from which he attempted to exert a weak and hesitant authority over what friend and foe alike contemptuously termed 'the kingdom of Bourges'. But with Joan's arrival, conditions rapidly improved: Orleans was relieved in May, Charles crowned in August. And though the Maid herself was soon to be captured, tried and burned, her example gave rise to a flood of national sentiment which, within twenty years, would lead to the liberation and unification of France.

No one can hope to explain Joan of Arc, and possibly we should not try: in mystery lies the secret of her appeal. Yet, even as paraphrased by hostile inquisitors, her common-sense realism emerges with an exceptional clarity that no amount of religious scepticism can deny:

> She replied that she confessed she brought news from God to her king; and that Our Lord would restore his kingdom to him, have him crowned at Rheims, and drive out his enemies. And that she was God's messenger in telling him that he must put her boldly to work, and that she would raise the siege of Orleans.
> She said also that she had said: All the kingdom. And that if my lord of Burgundy and the other subjects of the realm did not come to obedience, the king would make them do so by force.[100]

Clear objectives, logical objectives – and ones for which she was willing to pay with her life:

> Questioned ... if she believes that she is not bound to submit her words and deeds to the Church Militant or to any other than God,
> She answered: I will maintain what I have always said at my trial.
> And if I were to be condemned and saw the fire lit and the wood prepared and the executioner who was to burn me ready to cast me into the fire, still in the fire would I not say anything than I have said. And I will maintain what I have said until death.[101]

With these words, the end of the Middle Ages drew near. For, caught up though Joan was in visions of crusading ardour, hers was a voice that heralded different times, times in which the individual conscience would defy the will of the Church, and in which men would begin to declare that the sovereignty of the state could brook no opposition. In Italy and Bohemia, such notions had already gained widespread acceptance, and before another century had passed, they would be increasingly employed throughout the expanse of Europe. But Joan's was not the world of Machiavelli and the Renaissance, and neither was it that of Luther. Dying serene in the faith that 'God helping me, today I shall be with Him in Paradise',[102] she was the last of the medieval saints. And though her career did much to end chivalry, our memory of her does much to preserve it.

Footnotes

1 Gregory of Tours, tr. E. Bréhaut, *History of the Franks* (New York, Columbia University Press, 1916), 40–41.
2 The Venerable Bede, tr. Stevens and Giles, *The Ecclesiastical History of the English Nation* (London, J. M. Dent & Sons, 1910), 91.
3 Gregory of Tours, 50.
4 J. Crosland, tr., *Raoul de Cambrai* (London, Chatto & Windus, 1926), 46–7.
5 Gregory of Tours, 1.
6 *Ibid.*, 38.
7 *Ibid.*, 221–2.
8 *Ibid.*, 130.
9 *Ibid.*, 45.
10 *Ibid.*, 53.
11 *Ibid.*, 48.
12 *Ibid.*, 247.
13 *Ibid.*, 129.
14 *Ibid.*, 133.
15 H. Fichtenau, *The Carolingian Empire* (Oxford, Basil Blackwell, 1957), 60.
16 D. C. Munro, tr., *Translations and Reprints from the Original Sources of European History* (Philadelphia, University of Pennsylvania Press, 1900), VI, no. 5, 17.
17 Fichtenau, 98.
18 Einhard, tr. S. E. Turner, *The Life of Charlemagne* (Ann Arbor, The University of Michigan Press, 1960), 54.
19 *Ibid.*, 50–3.
20 M. Bloch, *Feudal Society* (London, Routledge & Kegan Paul, 1961), 39.
21 F. B. Luquiens, tr., *The Song of Roland* (New York, The Macmillan Company, 1952), 6.
22 *Ibid.*, 51.
23 *Ibid.*, 28.
24 *Ibid.*, 38–40.
25 *Ibid.*, 93.
26 *Ibid.*, 56.
27 *Ibid.*, 65.
28 *Ibid.*, 48.
29 *Ibid.*, 58.
30 Liudprand of Cremona, tr. F. A. Wright, *The Works of Liudprand of Cremona* (London, George Routledge & Sons, 1930), 231.
31 *Ibid.*, 217–18.
32 R. S. Hoyt, *Europe in the Middle Ages*, 2nd ed. (New York, Harcourt, Brace & World, 1966), 198–9.
33 *Ibid.*, 196.
34 Bloch, 87.
35 G. F. Whicher, tr., *The Goliard Poets* (New York, New Directions, 1949), 9.
36 *Ibid.*, 203.
37 O. J. Thatcher and E. H. McNeal, eds., *A Source Book for Mediaeval History* (New York, Charles Scribner's Sons, 1905), 572–3.
38 P. Lacroix, *France in the Middle Ages* (New York, Frederick Ungar Publishing Co., 1963), 101–2 (translation somewhat modified).
39 A. C. Krey, ed., *The First Crusade: The Accounts of Eye-Witnesses and Participants* (Princeton University Press, 1921), 99–100.
40 Robert of Clari, tr. E. H. McNeal, *The Conquest of Constantinople* (New York,

Columbia University Press, 1936), 67.
41 *Ibid.*, 101.
42 *Ibid.*, 112–13.
43 Odo of Deuil, tr. V. G. Berry, *De Profectione Ludovici* VII *in Orientem* (New York, Colombia University Press 1948), 65.
44 E. K. Kendall, ed., *Source Book of English History* (New York, The Macmillan Company, 1900), 65, 68–9.
45 Whicher, 107, 109, 111.
46 D. C. Douglas and G. W. Greenaway, *English Historical Documents* 1042–1189 (London, Eyre & Spottiswoode, 1953), II, 970–1.
47 *Ibid.*, 947–8.
48 Thatcher and McNeal, 585–6.
49 J. H. Mundy and P. Riesenburg, eds., *The Medieval Town* (Princeton, D. Van Nostrand Company, 1958), 115.
50 C. W. Jones, ed., *Medieval Literature in Translation* (London, Longmans, Green & Co., 1950), 606.
51 Kendall, 69, 70, 71.
52 Richard de Devizes, G. de Vinsauf and J. de Joinville, *Chronicles of the Crusades* (London, H. G. Bohn, 1848), 64.
53 Anna Comnena, *Alexiad* (London, Kegan Paul, Trench, Trubner & Company, 1928), 251.
54 D. C. Munro, tr., *Translations and Reprints from the Original Sources of European History* (Philadelphia, University of Pennsylvania Press, 1897), I, no. 4, 5.
55 *Ibid.*, I, no. 4, 10.
56 R. de Devizes, G. de Vinsauf and J. de Joinville, 271.
57 Usāmah Ibn-Munquidh, tr. P. K. Hitti, *An Arab-Syrian Gentleman and Warrior in the Period of the Crusades* (New York, Columbia University Press 1929), 161.
58 Douglas and Greenaway, II, 219.
59 Krey, 27–8.
60 *Ibid.*, 30–1.
61 *Ibid.*, 29–30.
62 G. G. Coulton, ed., *Life in the Middle Ages* (Cambridge University Press, 1929), 169–70, 172.
63 H. O. Taylor, *The Medieval Mind*, 4th

ed. (Cambridge, Mass., Harvard University Press, 1951), I, 412.
64 *Ibid.*, I, 426.
65 Luquiens, 40.
66 *Ibid.*, 60.
67 Andreas Capellanus, tr. J. J. Parry, *The Art of Love of Andreas Capellanus* (New York, Columbia University Press, 1941), 28.
68 *Ibid.*, 184–5.
69 P. Sabatier, *Life of St. Francis of Assisi* (New York, Charles Scribner's Sons, 1894), 305–6.
70 A. Kemp-Welch, tr. *Of the Tumbler of our Lady & Other Miracles* (London, Chatto & Windus, 1903), 4, 5, 18–19, 28–9.
71 C. Petit-Dutaillis, *The Feudal Monarchy in France and England* (London, Routledge & Kegan Paul, 1936), 316–17.
72 Marco Polo, tr. R. E. Latham, *The Travels of Marco Polo* (New York, Boni and Liveright, 1926), 3.
73 E. Panofsky, ed. and tr., *Abbot Suger on the Abbey Church of St. Denis* (Princeton University Press, 1946), 83.
74 *Ibid.*, 91.
75 C. H. Haskins, *The Rise of Universities* (New York, Henry Holt and Company, 1923), 104–5, 107–8.
76 J. de Joinville, tr. R. Hague, *The Life of St. Louis* (New York, Sheed and Ward, 1955), 35–6.
77 Dante Alighieri, tr. L. Binyon, *Paradiso* (London, Macmillan & Co., 1943), 395.
78 Petit-Dutaillis, 219.
79 E. Boutaric, *Saint Louis et Alfonse de Poitiers* (Paris, Henri Plon, 1870), 51.
80 Joinville, 28–9.
81 J. de Joinville, tr. F. Marzials, *Memoirs of the Crusades* (London, Everyman's Library, 1908), 277.
82 Joinville, tr. Hague, 25.
83 *Ibid.*, 37–8.
84 Petit-Dutaillis, 323.
85 *Ibid.*, 319.
86 W. Stubbs, *The Constitutional History of England* (Oxford, Clarendon Press, 1880), II, 120.

87 C. Stephenson and F. Marcham, eds., *Sources of English Constitutional History* (New York, Harper & Brothers, 1937), 148.
88 *Ibid.*, 205.
89 J. Huizinga, *The Waning of the Middle Ages* (London, E. Arnold & Co., 1924), 27.
90 J. Froissart, *Chronicles of England, France, Spain and the Adjoining Countries* (London, William Smith, 1839), I, 200.
91 C. T. Wood, *Philip the Fair and Boniface* VIII (New York, Holt, Rinehart and Winston, 1967), 85.
92 J. Michelet, *History of France* (New York, D. Appleton and Company, 1867), I, 358.
93 Wood, 3.
94 Froissart, I, 240, 242–3.
95 W. L. Warren, 'The Peasants' Revolt of 1381, Part Two,' *History Today*, XIII (1963), 50.
96 Froissart, II, 551–2.
97 *Ibid.*, I, 1.
98 *Ibid.*, I, 395.
99 *Ibid.*, I, 166.
100 W. S. Scott, ed. and tr., *The Trial of Joan of Arc* (London, The Folio Society, 1956), 135.
101 *Ibid.*, 162.
102 *Ibid.*, 171.

List of Dates

purchased the office from Benedict; and of Clement II (1046–1047), appointee of Henry III and first of the reformed popes

1035 The minor William the Conqueror becomes duke of Normandy

1040 Death, on pilgrimage to Jerusalem, of Fulk Nerra the Black, count of Anjou

1047 William the Conqueror wins the battle of Val ès Dunes, establishing his rule in Normandy

1066 Battle of Hastings; William crowned king of England (1066–1087)

1070 Formation and revolt of the commune of Le Mans

1075–1122 The Investiture Conflict, whose principal antagonists are Gregory VII (1073–1084) and Henry IV (1056–1106)

1095 Urban II preaches the First Crusade at the Council of Clermont

1098 *Carta Caritatis* written, founding document of the Cistercians

1099 Jerusalem falls to the forces of the First Crusade

1106 Charter of Henry I to Newcastle-upon-Tyne

1109 Death of St Anselm, archbishop of Canterbury and leading theologian of the day

1112 Uprising of the commune of Laon

1114 Foundation of Clairvaux, St Bernard's abbey

1137 Marriage of Louis VII (1137–1180) and Eleanor of Aquitaine; death of Louis VI (1108–1137)

1142 Death of Abelard

1147–1149 Second Crusade, preached by St Bernard and led by Louis VII and Conrad III of Germany

1151 Death of Suger of St Denis, one of the creators of Gothic

1152 Divorce of Louis VII and Eleanor of Aquitaine; marriage of Eleanor with Henry II (1154–1189)

1153 Death of St Bernard

1170 Martyrdom of Becket after outburst by Henry II

1187 Saladin recaptures Jerusalem

1189–1192 Third Crusade, led by Richard the Lion-Hearted (1189–1199), Philip Augustus (1180–1223) and the Emperor Frederick Barbarossa (1152–1190)

1202 Court of Philip Augustus condemns John (1199–1216) as contumacious vassal; all English lands in France declared forfeit

1204 Death of Eleanor of Aquitaine; Fourth Crusade takes Constantinople; last English strongholds in Normandy fall to French

1208 Albigensian Crusade preached by Innocent III (1198–1216), strongest of the medieval popes

1215 Barons force John to seal Magna Carta

1221 Death of St Dominic

1226 Death of St Francis of Assisi

1227 Death of Genghis Khan, founder of the Mongol Empire

1227–1228 Crusade of Frederick II

1241 Revolt of Hugh the Brown, count of La Marche, against Blanche of Castile and St Louis (1226–1270)

1248–1254 First Crusade of St Louis

1250 Death of Frederick II
1254 Consecration of choir at St Julian's of Le Mans
1265 Parliament of Simon de Montfort
1270 Death of St Louis while on his second Crusade
1274 Death of St Thomas Aquinas; Edward I (1272–1307) begins inquests that will lead to *Quo Warranto* proceedings
1275 Marco Polo arrives at court of Kublai Khan
1295 So-called 'Model Parliament' of Edward I
1296 In *Clericis Laicos* Boniface VIII (1294–1303) forbids secular taxation of clerics; Edward I and Philip the Fair (1285–1314) respond sharply
1297 Canonization of St Louis
1302 Boniface VIII issues *Unam Sanctam*, strong statement of papal powers
1303 Nogaret and Italian troops storm papal residence at Anagni, capturing Boniface VIII who dies a month later
1305–1378 So-called Babylonian Captivity of the Church at Avignon
1315–1317 Bad harvests lead to serious famine throughout Europe
1321 Death of Dante
1337–1453 Hundred Years War
1346 Edward III (1327–1377) beats French at battle of Crécy
1348 Black Death becomes widespread in Europe
1356 Black Prince beats French at battle of Poitiers; John the Good (1350–1364) captured
1358 The Jacquerie, rebellion of French peasants
1378–1415 The Great Schism
1381 The Peasants' Revolt in England
1392 Charles VI (1380–1422) goes insane
1407 Assassination of Louis, duke of Orleans, an event that leads to French civil wars
1415 Henry V (1413–1422) beats French at battle of Agincourt
1420 Treaty of Troyes excludes Dauphin from French succession, granting it to heir of Henry V and Catherine of Valois
1429 Joan of Arc relieves siege of Orleans and has Charles VII (1422–1461) crowned at Reims
1431 Joan burned as heretic in marketplace at Rouen
1453 Bordeaux falls to French forces, ending the Hundred Years War

List of Illustrations

Bibliography

Sources

Abelard, tr. J. T. Muckle, *The Story of Abelard's Adversities*; Toronto: The Pontifical Institute of Medieval Studies, 1954.

Andreas Capellanus, tr. J. J. Parry, *The Art of Courtly Love of Andreas Capellanus*; New York: Columbia University Press, 1941.

Bede, The Venerable, tr. Stevens and Giles, *The Ecclesiastical History of the English Nation*; London: Everyman's Library (J. M. Dent & Sons), 1910.

Comnena, Anna, *Alexiad*; London: Kegan Paul, Trench, Trubner & Company, 1928.

Douglas, D. C., ed., *English Historical Documents 1042-1189*, Vol. II; London: Eyre & Spottiswoode, 1953.

Einhard, tr. S. E. Turner, *The Life of Charlemagne*; Ann Arbor: The University of Michigan Press, 1960.

Froissart, J., *Chronicles of England, France, Spain and the Adjoining Countries* (2 vols); London: William Smith, 1839.

Gregory, bishop of Tours, tr. E. Bréhaut, *History of the Franks*; New York: Columbia University Press, 1916.

Henderson, E. F., ed., *Select Historical Documents of the Middle Ages*; London: G. Bell & Sons, 1896.

Joinville, Jean sire de, tr. R. Hague, *The Life of St Louis*; London: Sheed and Ward, 1955.

Jones, C. W., ed., *Medieval Literature in Translation*; London: Longmans, Green & Co., 1950.

Kendall, E. K., ed., *Source Book of English History*; New York: The Macmillan Company, 1900.

Krey, A. C., ed., *The First Crusade: The Accounts of Eye-Witnesses and Participants*; London: Humphrey Milford, Oxford University Press, 1921.

Liudprand of Cremona, tr. F. A. Wright, *The Works of Liudprand of Cremona*; London: George Routledge & Sons, 1930.

Odo of Deuil, tr. V. G. Berry, *De Profectione Ludovici VII in Orientem*; New York: Columbia University Press, 1948.

Panofsky, E., ed., *Abbot Suger on the Abbey Church of St.Denis and its Art Treasures*; Princeton University Press, 1946.

Polo, Marco, tr. R. E. Latham, *The Travels of Marco Polo*; New York: Boni and Liveright, 1926.

Raoul de Cambrai, tr. Jessie Crosland; London: Chatto & Windus, 1926.

Richard de Devizes, G. de Vinsauf, J. de Joinville, *Chronicles of the Crusades*; London: H. G. Bohn, 1848.

Robert of Clari, tr. E. H. McNeal, *The Conquest of Constantinople*; New York: Columbia University Press, 1936.

Scott, W. S., ed., *The Trial of Joan of Arc*; London: The Folio Society, 1956.

The Song of Roland, tr. F. B. Luquiens; New York: The Macmillan Company, 1952.

Stephenson, C. and Marcham, F., eds., *Sources of English Constitutional History*; New York and London: Harper & Brothers, 1937.

Usāmah Ibn-Munquidh, tr. P. K. Hitti, *An Arab-Syrian Gentleman and Warrior in the Period of the Crusades*; New York: Columbia University Press, 1929.

Waddell, H., ed., *The Wandering Scholars* (7th ed.); London: Constable & Co., 1934.

Walter of Henley, tr. E. Lamond, *Walter of Henley's Husbandry*, London: Longmans, Green & Co., 1890.

Whicher, G. F., ed., *The Goliard Poets*; New York: New Directions, 1949.

General

Aston, M., *The Fifteenth Century: The Prospect of Europe*; London: Thames and Hudson, 1968.

Bark, W. C., *Origins of the Medieval World*; Stanford University Press, 1958.

Barraclough, G., ed., *Medieval Germany, 911–1250* (2 vols); Oxford: Basil Blackwell, 1938.

Blair, P. H., *An Introduction to Anglo-Saxon England*; Cambridge University Press, 1962.

Brønsted, J., *The Vikings*; London: Penguin Books, 1960.

Brooke, C., *Europe in the Central Middle Ages 962–1154*; London: Longmans, Green & Co., 1964.

Cam, H. M., *England Before Elizabeth*; London: Hutchinson University Library, 1950.

Cambridge Mediaeval History (8 vols); Cambridge University Press, 1911–36.

Churchill, W. S., *The Birth of Britain*; New York: Dodd, Mead, 1956.

Davis, H. W. C., *Medieval Europe* (2nd ed.); London: Home University Library (Oxford University Press), 1960.

Dawson, C., *The Making of Europe*; London: Sheed and Ward, 1932.
    Religion and the Rise of Western Culture; London: Sheed and Ward, 1950.

Duby, G., *The Making of the Christian West, 980–1140*; Geneva: Skira, 1967.

Duby, G. and Mandrou, R., *A History of French Civilization*; New York: Random House, 1964.

Evans, J., *The Flowering of the Middle Ages*; London: Thames and Hudson, 1966.

Fichtenau, H., *The Carolingian Empire*; Oxford: Basil Blackwell, 1957.

Glotz, G., ed., *Histoire générale . . . Histoire du moyen âge* (10 vols); Paris: Presses Universitaires de France, 1928–45.

Hales, J., Highfield, R., and Smalley, B., eds., *Europe in the late Middle Ages*; London: Faber and Faber, 1965.

Haskins, C. H., *The Normans in History*; Boston and New York: Houghton-Mifflin, 1915.

Hay, D., *Europe in the Fourteenth and Fifteenth Centuries*; London: Longmans, Green & Co., 1966.

Heer, F., *The Medieval World*; London: George Weidenfeld & Nicolson, 1961.
The Holy Roman Empire; London: George Weidenfeld & Nicolson, 1968.

Jones, A. H. M., *The Decline of the Ancient World*; London: Longmans, Green & Co., 1966.

Lacroix, P., *France in the Middle Ages*; New York: Frederick Ungar Publishing Co., 1963.

Lavisse, E., ed., *Histoire de France depuis les origines jusqu'à la Révolution* (9 vols); Paris: Librairie Hachette et Cie, 1900–11.

LeGoff, J., *La civilisation de l'Occident médiéval*; Paris: Éditions Arthaud, 1967.

Lewis, A. R., *The Development of Southern French and Catalan Society 718–1050*; Austin: University of Texas Press, 1965.

Lopez, R. S., *The Birth of Europe*; New York and Philadelphia: M. Evans and Lippincott, 1967.

Lot, F., *The End of the Ancient World and the Beginnings of the Middle Ages*; London: Routledge & Kegan Paul, 1931.

Moss, H. St L. B., *The Birth of the Middle Ages 395–814*; Oxford University Press, 1935.

Oxford History of England; Oxford University Press:
Stenton, F., *Anglo-Saxon England* (2nd ed.), 1947.
Poole, A. L., *From Domesday Book to Magna Carta* (2nd ed.), 1955.
Powicke, F. M., *The Thirteenth Century*, 1953.
McKisack, M., *The Fourteenth Century 1307–1399*, 1959.
Jacob, E. F., *The Fifteenth Century 1399–1485*, 1961.

Pirenne, H., *Mohammed and Charlemagne*; New York: W. W. Norton & Company, 1939.

Previté-Orton, C. W., *The Shorter Cambridge Mediaeval History* (2 vols); Cambridge University Press, 1952.

Southern, R. W., *The Making of the Middle Ages*; London: Hutchinson University Library, 1953.

Thrupp, S. L., ed., *Change in Medieval Society*; New York: Appleton-Century-Crofts, 1964.

Trevor-Roper, H., *The Rise of Christian Europe*; London: Thames and Hudson, 1965.

Wallace-Hadrill, J. M., *The Barbarian West 400–1000*; London: Hutchinson University Library, 1952.

The Church and Heresy

Barraclough, G., *The Medieval Papacy*; London: Thames and Hudson, 1968.

Boase, T. S. R., *Boniface VIII*; London: Constable & Co., 1933.

Brooke, Z. N., *The English Church and the Papacy from the Conquest to the Reign of John*; Cambridge University Press, 1931.

Cohn, N., *The Pursuit of the Millennium*; London: Secker & Warburg, 1957.

Creighton, M., *A History of the Papacy from the Great Schism to the Sack of Rome* (6 vols); London: Longmans, Green & Co., 1897.

Digard, G., *Philippe le bel et le Saint-Siège de 1285 à 1304* (2 vols); Paris: Librairie du Recueil Sirey, 1936.

Evans, J., *Monastic Life at Cluny*; London: Oxford University Press, 1931.

Fliche, A., and Martin, V., *Histoire de l'église depuis les origines jusqu'à nos jours* (vols. IV–XV); Paris: Bloud & Gay, 1934 et seq.

Flick, A. C., *The Decline of the Medieval Church* (2 vols); London: Kegan Paul, Trench, Trubner & Co., 1930.

The Rise of the Mediaeval Church; New York: Burt Franklin Reprints, 1959.

Gebhart, E., *Mystics and Heretics in Italy*; New York: Alfred Knopf, 1922.

Godfrey, C. J., *The Church in Anglo-Saxon England*; Cambridge University Press, 1962.

Hughes, P., *A History of the Church* (3 vols); London: Sheed and Ward, 1934–47.

Knowles, D., *The Monastic Order in England*; Cambridge University Press, 1940.

The Religious Orders in England (3 vols); Cambridge University Press, 1950–9.

Lea, H. C., *A History of the Inquisition of the Middle Ages* (3 vols); New York: Harper and Brothers, 1888.

Mollat, G., *The Popes at Avignon 1305–1378*; London: Thomas Nelson & Sons, 1963.

Oldenbourg, Z., *Massacre at Montségur*; London: George Weidenfeld & Nicolson, 1961.

Robbins, R. H., *The Encyclopedia of Witchcraft and Demonology*; New York: Crown Publishers Inc., 1959.

Tellenbach, G., *Church, State and Society at the Time of the Investiture Contest*; Oxford: Basil Blackwell, 1959.

Troeltsch, E., *The Social Teachings of the Christian Churches*; London: George Allen & Unwin, 1931.

Ullmann, W., *The Growth of Papal Government in the Middle Ages* (2nd ed.); London: Methuen & Co., 1962.

Vacandard, E., *The Inquisition* (2nd ed.); New York: Longmans, Green & Co., 1921.

Wood, C. T., *Philip the Fair and Boniface VIII*; New York: Holt, Rinehart and Winston, 1967.

Cultural and Intellectual

Adams, H., *Mont-Saint-Michel and Chartres*; Boston: Houghton-Mifflin, 1922.

Bennett, H. S., *Chaucer and the Fifteenth Century*; Oxford University Press, 1947.

The Pastons and their England; Cambridge University Press, 1922.

Brandt, W., *The Shape of Medieval History: Studies in Modes of Perception*; New Haven and London: Yale University Press, 1966.

Carlyle, R. W. & A. J., *A History of Mediaeval Political Theory in the West* (6 vols); Edinburgh and London: William Blackwood & Sons, 1903–36.

Chaney, E. F., *François Villon in his Environment*; Oxford: Basil Blackwell, 1946.

Cochrane, C. N., *Christianity and Classical Culture* (rev. ed.); Oxford University Press, 1944.
Copleston, F. C., *A History of Philosophy* (vol. II): *Medieval Philosophy: Augustine to Scotus*; London: Penguin Books, 1950.
Medieval Philosophy; London: Methuen & Co., 1952.
Duckett, E., *Alcuin, Friend of Charlemagne*; New York: The Macmillan Company, 1951.
Death and Life in the Tenth Century; Ann Arbor: University of Michigan Press, 1967.
The Gateway to the Middle Ages; New York: The Macmillan Company, 1938.
The Wandering Saints of the Early Middle Ages; New York: W. W. Norton & Company, Inc., 1964.
Gilson, E., *Heloise and Abelard*; Chicago: H. Regnery Co., 1951.
History of Christian Philosophy in the Middle Ages; New York: Random House, 1955.
The Mystical Theology of St Bernard; London: Sheed and Ward, 1940.
The Philosophy of St Thomas Aquinas (2nd ed., rev.); London: B. Herder Book Co., 1937.
Reason and Revelation in the Middle Ages; New York: Charles Scribner's Sons, 1938.
Haskins, C. H., *The Renaissance of the Twelfth Century*; Cambridge, Mass.: Harvard University Press, 1927.
The Rise of Universities; New York: Henry Holt & Company, 1923.
Heer, F., *The Intellectual History of Europe*; New York: World Publishing Company, 1966.
Huizinga, J., *The Waning of the Middle Ages*; London: E. Arnold & Co., 1924.
Jaeger, W., *Early Christianity and Greek Paideia*; Cambridge, Mass.: Harvard University Press, 1961.
Kelly, A., *Eleanor of Aquitaine and the Four Kings*; Cambridge, Mass.: Harvard University Press, 1950.
Knowles, D., *The Evolution of Medieval Thought*; Baltimore: Helicon Press, 1962.
The Historian and Character; Cambridge University Press, 1963.
Saints and Scholars; Cambridge University Press, 1962.
Laistner, M. L. W., *Christianity and Pagan Culture in the Later Roman Empire*; Ithaca: Cornell University Press, 1951.
Thought and Letters in Western Europe A.D. *500 to 900* (new ed.); Ithaca: Cornell University Press, 1957.
Langlois, Ch.-V., *La connaissance de la nature et du monde au moyen âge*; Paris: Librairie Hachette et Cie, 1911.
Leclercq, J., *The Love of Learning and the Desire for God*; New York: Fordham University Press, 1961.
Leff, G., *Paris and Oxford Universities in the Thirteenth and Fourteenth Centuries*, New York: John Wiley & Sons, Inc., 1968.
Lewis, C. S., *The Allegory of Love*; Oxford University Press, 1936.
The Discarded Image; Cambridge University Press, 1964.
Lovejoy, A. O., *The Great Chain of Being*; Cambridge, Mass.: Harvard University Press, 1936.

McIlwain, C. H., *The Growth of Political Thought in the West*; New York: The Macmillan Company, 1932.

Mâle, E., *Religious Art in France of the Thirteenth Century*; New York: E. P. Dutton & Company, 1913.

Painter, S., *French Chivalry*; Baltimore: Johns Hopkins University Press, 1940.

Panofsky, E., *Gothic Architecture and Scholasticism*; Latrobe, Penna.: Archabbey Press, 1951.

Rashdall, H. (rev. by F. M. Powicke and A. B. Emden), *The Universities of Europe in the Middle Ages* (3 vols.); Oxford University Press, 1936.

Rougement, D. de, *Passion and Society*; London: Faber and Faber, 1956.

Smalley, B., *The Study of the Bible in the Middle Ages*; Oxford: Basil Blackwell, 1952.

Taylor, H. O., *The Mediaeval Mind* (2 vols, 4th ed.); London: Macmillan & Co., 1927.

Ullmann, W., *A History of Political Thought: The Middle Ages*; London: Penguin Books, 1965.

    Principles of Government and Politics in the Middle Ages; London: Methuen & Co., 1961.

Economic and Social

Ariès, P., *Centuries of Childhood*; London: Jonathan Cape, 1962.

Bennett, H. S., *Life on the English Manor*; Cambridge University Press, 1937.

Bloch, M., *Feudal Society*; London: Routledge & Kegan Paul, 1961.

    French Rural History; Berkeley and Los Angeles: University of California Press, 1966.

    Seigneurie française et manoir anglais; Paris: Armand Colin, 1960.

Boissonade, P., *Life and Work in Medieval Europe*; London: Kegan Paul, Trench, Trubner & Co., 1924.

Brown, R. A., *English Medieval Castles*; London: Batsford, 1954.

Clapham, J. H. *et al.*, eds., *The Cambridge Economic History* (vols I–III); Cambridge University Press, 1941–61.

Coulton, G. G., *The Black Death*; New York: J. Cape & H. Smith, 1930.

    Medieval Panorama; Cambridge University Press, 1938.

    The Medieval Scene; Cambridge University Press, 1930.

    The Medieval Village. Cambridge University Press, 1925.

    Social Life in Britain from the Conquest to the Reformation; Cambridge University Press, 1918.

Davis, W. S., *Life on a Medieval Barony*; New York and London: Harper and Brothers, 1923.

Dill, S., *Roman Society in Gaul in the Merovingian Age*; London: Macmillan & Co., 1926.

Dopsch, A., *The Economic and Social Foundations of European Civilization*; London: Kegan Paul, Trench, Trubner & Co., 1937.

Duby, G., *Rural Economy and Country Life in the Medieval West*; Columbia, S. C.: University of South Carolina Press, 1968.

Evans, J., *Dress in Mediaeval France*; Oxford University Press, 1952.
   Life in Mediaeval France; London: Oxford University Press, 1925.
Franklin, A., *La vie privée au temps des premiers Capétiens* (2 vols); Paris: Emile-Paul, 1911.
Gail, M., *Avignon in Flower, 1309–1403*; Boston: Houghton-Mifflin, 1965.
Holmes, U. T., *Daily Living in the Twelfth Century*; Madison: University of Wisconsin Press, 1952.
Homans, G. C., *English Villagers of the Thirteenth Century*; Cambridge, Mass.: Harvard University Press, 1940.
Kerr, A. B., *Jacques Cœur, Merchant Prince of the Middle Ages*; New York: Charles Scribner's Sons, 1927.
Latouche, R., *The Birth of Western Economy*; London: Methuen & Co., 1961.
   From Caesar to Charlemagne; New York: Barnes & Noble, Inc., 1968.
Loyn, H. R., *Anglo-Saxon England and the Norman Conquest*; New York: St Martin's Press, 1962.
Lot, F., *L'art militaire et les armées au moyen âge en Europe et dans le Proche Orient*; Paris: Payot, 1946.
Luchaire, A., *Social France at the Time of Philip Augustus*; London: J. Murray, 1912.
Myers, A. R., *England in the Late Middle Ages 1307–1536*; London: Penguin Books, 1952.
Oman, C. W. C., *The Art of War in the Middle Ages* (2nd ed., rev.); Ithaca: Cornell University Press, 1953.
Painter, S., *Medieval Society*; Ithaca: Cornell University Press, 1951.
Pirenne, H., *Belgian Democracy*; Manchester University Press, 1915.
   Economic and Social History of Medieval Europe; London: Kegan Paul, Trench, Trubner & Co., 1936.
   Medieval Cities; Princeton University Press, 1925.
Power, E., *Medieval People*; London: Methuen & Co., 1924.
   The Wool Trade in English Medieval History; London: Oxford University Press, 1941.
Powicke, F. M., *The Christian Life in the Middle Ages*; Oxford University Press, 1933.
Runciman, S., *A History of the Crusades* (3 vols); Cambridge University Press, 1951–54.
Setton, K., ed., *A History of the Crusades* (2 vols); Philadelphia: University of Pennsylvania Press, 1955–62.
Stenton, D. M., *English Society in the Early Middle Ages 1066–1307*; London: Penguin Books, 1952.
Trevelyan, G. M., *England in the Age of Wycliffe* (4th ed.); London: Longmans, Green & Co., 1909.
Uden, G., *A Dictionary of Chivalry*; New York: Thomas Y. Crowell Company, 1968.
Warner, P., *Sieges of the Middle Ages*; London: G. Bell & Sons, 1968.
White, L. jr., *Medieval Technology and Social Change*; Oxford University Press, 1962.
Whitelock, D., *The Beginnings of English Society*; London: Penguin Books, 1952.

Institutional and Political

Avout, J. d', *La querelle des Armagnacs et des Bourguignes*; Paris: Gallimard, 1943.

Barraclough, G., *The Origins of Modern Germany* (2nd ed.); New York: G. P. Putnam's Sons, 1963.

Bloch, M., *Les rois thaumaturges*; Strasbourg: Librairie Istra, 1924.

Bryce, J., *The Holy Roman Empire* (new ed.); London: Macmillan & Co., 1904.

Cazelles, R., *La société politique et la crise de la royauté sous Philippe de Valois*; Paris: Librairie d'Argences, 1958.

Duby, G., *La société aux XIe et XIIe siècles dans la région mâconnaise*; Paris: Armand Colin, 1953.

Fawtier, R., *The Capetian Kings of France;* London: Macmillan & Co., 1960.

Granshof, F., *Feudalism*; London: Longmans, Green & Co., 1952.

Kantorowicz, E., *Frederick the Second, 1194–1250*; New York: Frederick Ungar Publishing Co., 1957.

Kern, F., *Kingship and Law in the Middle Ages*; Oxford: Basil Blackwell, 1956.

Lewis, P. S., *France in the Later Middle Ages*; New York: St Martin's Press, 1967.

Lot, F., and Fawtier, R., *Histoire des institutions françaises au moyen âge* (3 vols); Paris: Presses Universitaires de France, 1957–62.

Luchaire, A., *Les communes françaises*; Paris: Librairie Hachette et Cie, 1911.

Perroy, E., *The Hundred Years War*; London: Eyre & Spottiswoode, 1951.

Petit-Dutaillis, C., *The Feudal Monarchy in France and England*; London: Routledge & Kegan Paul, 1936.

Rowse, A. L., *Bosworth Field*; Garden City, N. Y.: Doubleday & Company, Inc., 1966.

Sayles, G. O., *The Medieval Foundations of England* (2nd ed.); London: Methuen & Co., 1950.

Tillemont, Le Nain de, *Vie de Saint Louis* (6 vols); Paris: Chez Jules Renouard et Cie, 1847–51.

Vaughan, R., *John the Fearless*; London: Longmans, Green & Co., 1966.
   Philip the Bold: The Formation of the Burgundian State; Oxford University Press, 1962.

Vermeesch, A., *Essai sur les origines et la signification de la commune dans le nord de la France (XIe et XIIe siècles)*; Heule: UGA, 1966.

Wallace-Hadrill, J. M., *The Long-Haired Kings*; London: Methuen & Co., 1962.

Wood, C. T., *The French Apanages and the Capetian Monarchy 1225–1328*; Cambridge, Mass.: Harvard University Press, 1966.

Index

INDEX